The Selected Works of Nikita Khrushchev

The Selected Works of Nikita Khrushchev

The Selected Works of The Selected Works of Nikita Khrushchev

ISBN: 978-1-304-83945-9

This Edition First Printed June 2021

Table of Contents

Obituary of G.M. Dimitrov

Georgi Mikhailovitch Dimitrov was born on June 18, 1882, in the town of Radomir, of a proletarian revolutionary family. When he was only 15 years old, the young Dimitrov, working as a compositor in a print shop, joined the revolutionary movement and took an active part in the work of the oldest Bulgarian trade union of printers.

In 1902, Dimitrov joined the Bulgarian Workers' Social Democratic Party. He actively combated revisionism on the side of the revolutionary Marxist wing of Tesnyaki led by Dimitri Blagoyev.

The self-sacrificing revolutionary struggle of Dimitrov earned him the warm love of the revolutionary workers of Bulgaria, who, in 1905, elected him secretary of the Alliance of Revolutionary Trade Associations of Bulgaria. In that post he remained right up to 1923, when that alliance was disbanded by the fascists.

While leading the struggle of the Bulgarian proletariat, Dimitrov displayed courage and staunchness in the revolutionary struggles, was repeatedly arrested and persecuted. In the September armed uprising of 1923 in Bulgaria he headed the Central Revolutionary Committee, set an example of revolutionary fearlessness, unflinching staunchness and devotion to the cause of the working class. For his leadership of the armed uprising in 1923 the fascist court sentenced Dimitrov in his absence to death. In 1926, after the provocative trial, engineered by the fascists, against the leadership of the Communist Party, Dimitrov was again sentenced to death in his absence.

Compelled, in 1923, to emigrate from Bulgaria, Dimitrov led the life of a professional revolutionary. He worked actively in the Executive Committee of the Communist International.

In 1933, he was arrested in Berlin for revolutionary activity. During the Leipzig Trial, Dimitrov became the standard-bearer of the struggle against fascism and imperialist war. His heroic conduct in the court, the words of wrath which he flung in the face of the fascists, exposing their infamous provocation in connection with the Reichstag fire, unmasked the fascist provocateurs and roused new millions of workers throughout the world to the struggle against fascism.

In 1935, Dimitrov was elected General Secretary of the Executive Committee of the Communist International. He waged a persistent struggle for the creation and consolidation of the united proletarian and popular front for the struggle against fascism, against the war which the fascist rulers of Germany, Japan and Italy were preparing. He called untiringly on the masses of the working people of all countries to rally around the Communist Parties in order to bar the way to the Fascist aggressors.

Dimitrov did great work in the ranks of the international Communist movement in forging the leading cadres of Communist Parties loyal to the great teachings of Marxism-Leninism, to the principles of proletarian internationalism, to the cause of the defense of the interests of the people's masses in their respective countries.

During the Second World War, Georgi Dimitrov called on the Communists to head the national-liberation anti-fascist movement, and tirelessly worked at organizing all patriotic forces for the rout of the fascist invaders. He led the struggle of the Bulgarian Workers' Party (Communists) and all Bulgarian patriots who rose in arms against the German-fascist invaders.

For his outstanding services in the struggle against fascism he was, in 1945, awarded the Order of Lenin by the Presidium of the Supreme Soviet of the U.S.S.R.

After the defeat of fascist Germany, Georgi Mikhailovitch Dimitrov led the building of the new People's Democratic Republic of Bulgaria, and laid the foundation for the eternal friendship between the Bulgarian people and the peoples of the Soviet Union. Untiringly working for the consolidation of the united anti-imperialist camp and the rallying of all democratic forces, Georgi Mikhailovitch Dimitrov mercilessly exposed the betrayal of the cause of Socialism and the united anti-imperialist front by Tito's nationalist clique.

In the person of Dimitrov, the working people of the whole

world have lost an ardent fighter, who gave all his heroic life to the supreme service of the cause of the working class, the cause of Communism. The death of Dimitrov is a great loss to the whole international working class and Communist movement, to all fighters for lasting peace and a people's democracy. By his self-sacrificing struggle in the ranks of the working-class movement, by his boundless devotion to the great teachings of Lenin and Stalin, Dimitrov earned the warm love of the working people of the whole world.

The life of Dimitrov, loyal comrade-in-arms of Lenin and Stalin, staunch revolutionary and anti-fascist champion, will serve as an inspiring example to all fighters for the cause of peace and democracy, for Communism.

Farewell, our dear friend and comrade-in-arms!

Signed,

Andreyev, Beria, Bulganin, Voroshilov, Kaganovitch, Kosygin, Malenkov, Mikoyan, Molotov, Ponomarenko, Popov, Pospelov, Stalin, Suslov, Khrushchev, Shvernik, Shkiryatov.

Speech to 20th Congress of the C.P.S.U.

At the Twentieth Congress of the CPSU February 24-25 1956, Khrushchev delivered a report in which he denounced Stalin's crimes and the 'cult of personality' surrounding Stalin. This speech would ultimately trigger a world-wide split in the official Communist parties.

Comrades! In the Party Central Committee's report at the 20th Congress and in a number of speeches by delegates to the Congress, as also formerly during Plenary CC/CPSU [Central Committee of the Communist Party of the Soviet Union] sessions, quite a lot has been said about the cult of the individual and about its harmful consequences.

After Stalin's death, the Central Committee began to implement a policy of explaining concisely and consistently that it is impermissible and foreign to the spirit of Marxism-Leninism to elevate one person, to transform him into a superman possessing supernatural characteristics, akin to those of a god. Such a man supposedly knows everything, sees everything, thinks for everyone, can do anything, is infallible in his behavior.

Such a belief about a man, and specifically about Stalin, was cultivated among us for many years. The objective of the present report is not a thorough evaluation of Stalin's life and activity. Concerning Stalin's merits, an entirely sufficient number of books, pamphlets and studies had already been written in his lifetime. The role of Stalin in the preparation and execution of the Socialist Revolution, in the Civil War, and in the fight for the construction of socialism in our country, is universally known. Everyone knows it well.

At present, we are concerned with a question which has immense importance for the Party now and for the future – with how the cult of the person of Stalin has been gradually growing, the cult which became at a certain specific stage the source of a whole series of exceedingly serious and grave perversions of Party principles, of Party democracy, of revolutionary legality.

Because not all as yet realize fully the practical consequences resulting from the cult of the individual, [or] the great harm caused by violation of the principle of collective Party direction and by the accumulation of immense and limitless power in the hands of one person, the Central Committee considers it absolutely necessary to make material pertaining to this matter available to the 20th Congress of the Communist Party of the Soviet Union.

Allow me first of all to remind you how severely the classics of Marxism-Leninism denounced every manifestation of the cult of the individual. In a letter to the German political worker Wilhelm Bloss, [Karl] Marx stated: "From my antipathy to any cult of the individual, I never made public during the existence of the [1st] International the numerous addresses from various countries which recognized my merits and which annoyed me. I did not even reply to them, except sometimes to rebuke their authors. [Fredrich] Engels and I first joined the secret society of Communists on the condition that everything making for superstitious worship of authority would be deleted from its statute. [Ferdinand] Lassalle subsequently did quite the opposite."

Sometime later Engels wrote: "Both Marx and I have always been against any public manifestation with regard to individuals, with the exception of cases when it had an important purpose. We most strongly opposed such manifestations which during our lifetime concerned us personally."

The great modesty of the genius of the Revolution, Vladimir Ilyich Lenin, is known. Lenin always stressed the role of the people as the creator of history, the directing and organizational roles of the Party as a living and creative organism, and also the role of the Central Committee.

Marxism does not negate the role of the leaders of the working class in directing the revolutionary liberation movement.

While ascribing great importance to the role of the leaders and organizers of the masses, Lenin at the same time mercilessly stigmatized every manifestation of the cult of the individual, inexorably combated [any] foreign-to-Marxism views about a "hero" and a "crowd," and countered all efforts to oppose a "hero" to the masses and to the people.

Lenin taught that the Party's strength depends on its indissoluble unity with the masses, on the fact that behind the Party follows the people – workers, peasants, and the intelligentsia. Lenin said, "Only he who believes in the people, [he] who submerges himself in the fountain of the living creativeness of the people, will win and retain power."

Lenin spoke with pride about the Bolshevik Communist Party as the leader and teacher of the people. He called for the presentation of all the most important questions before the opinion of knowledgeable workers, before the opinion of their Party. He said: "We believe in it, we see in it the wisdom, the honor, and the conscience of our epoch."

Lenin resolutely stood against every attempt aimed at belittling or weakening the directing role of the Party in the structure of the Soviet state. He worked out Bolshevik principles of Party direction and norms of Party life, stressing that the guiding principle of Party leadership is its collegiality. Already during the pre-Revolutionary years, Lenin called the Central Committee a collective of leaders and the guardian and interpreter of Party principles. "During the period between congresses," Lenin pointed out, "the Central Committee guards and interprets the principles of the Party."

Underlining the role of the Central Committee and its authority, Vladimir Ilyich pointed out: "Our Central Committee constituted itself as a closely centralized and highly authoritative group."

During Lenin's life the Central Committee was a real expression of collective leadership: of the Party and of the nation. Being a militant Marxist-revolutionist, always unyielding in matters of principle, Lenin never imposed his views upon his co-workers by force. He tried to convince. He patiently explained his opinions to others. Lenin always diligently saw to it that the norms of Party life were realized, that Party statutes were enforced, that Party congresses and Plenary sessions of the Central Committee took place at their proper intervals.

In addition to V. I. Lenin's great accomplishments for the victory of the working class and of the working peasants, for the victory of our Party and for the application of the ideas of scientific Communism to life, his acute mind expressed itself also in this. [Lenin] detected in Stalin in time those negative characteristics which resulted later in grave consequences. Fearing the future fate of the Party and of the Soviet nation, V. I. Lenin made a completely correct characterization of Stalin. He pointed out that it was necessary to consider transferring Stalin from the position of [Party] General Secretary because Stalin was excessively rude, did not have a proper attitude toward his comrades, and was capricious and abused his power.

In December **1922**, in a letter to the Party Congress, Vladimir Ilyich wrote: "After taking over the position of General Secretary, comrade Stalin accumulated immeasurable power in his hands and I am not certain whether he will be always able to use this power with the required care."

This letter – a political document of tremendous importance, known in the Party's history as Lenin's "Testament" - was distributed among [you] delegates to [this] 20th Party Congress. You have read it and will undoubtedly read it again more than once. You might reflect on Lenin's plain words, in which expression is given to Vladimir Ilyich's anxiety concerning the Party, the people, the state, and the future direction of Party policy.

Vladimir Ilyich said:

"Stalin is excessively rude, and this defect, which can be freely tolerated in our midst and in contacts among us Communists, becomes a defect which cannot be tolerated in one holding the position of General Secretary. Because of this, I propose that the comrades consider the method by which Stalin would be removed from this position and by which another man would be selected for it, a man who, above all, would differ from Stalin in only one quality, namely, greater tolerance, greater loyalty, greater kindness and more considerate attitude toward the comrades, a less capricious temper, etc."

This document of Lenin's was made known to the delegates at the 13th Party Congress, who discussed the question of transferring Stalin from the position of General Secretary. The delegates declared themselves in favor of retaining Stalin in this post, hoping that he would heed Vladimir Ilyich's critical remarks and would be able to overcome the defects which caused Lenin serious anxiety.

Comrades! The Party Congress should become acquainted with two new documents, which confirm Stalin's character as already outlined by Vladimir Ilyich Lenin in his "Testament." These documents are a letter from Nadezhda Konstantinovna Krupskaya to [Lev] Kamenev, who was at that time head of the Politburo, and a personal letter from Vladimir Ilyich Lenin to Stalin.

I will now read these documents:

"LEV BORISOVICH!

"Because of a short letter which I had written in words dictated to me by Vladimir Ilyich by permission of the doctors, Stalin allowed himself yesterday an unusually rude outburst directed at me.

This is not my first day in the Party. During all these 30 years I have never heard one word of rudeness from any comrade. The Party's and Ilyich's business is no less dear to me than to Stalin. I need maximum self-control right now. What one can and what one cannot discuss with Ilyich I know better than any doctor, because I know what makes him nervous and what does not. In any case I know [it] better than Stalin. I am turning to you and to Grigory [Zinoviev] as much closer comrades of V[ladimir] I[lyich]. I beg you to protect me from rude interference with my private life and from vile invectives and threats. I have no doubt what the Control Commission's unanimous decision [in this matter], with which Stalin sees fit to threaten me, will be. However I have neither strength nor time to waste on this foolish quarrel. And I am a human being and my nerves are strained to the utmost.

"N. KRUPSKAYA"

Nadezhda Konstantinovna wrote this letter on December 23, 1922. After two and a half months, in March 1923, Vladimir Ilyich Lenin sent Stalin the following letter:

"TO COMRADE STALIN (COPIES FOR: KAMENEV AND ZINOVIEV):

"Dear comrade Stalin!

"You permitted yourself a rude summons of my wife to the telephone and a rude reprimand of her. Despite the fact that she told you that she agreed to forget what was said, nevertheless Zinoviev and Kamenev heard about it from her. I have no intention to forget so easily that which is being done against me. I need not stress here that I consider as directed against me that which is being done against my wife. I ask you, therefore, that you weigh carefully whether you are agreeable to retracting your words and apologizing, or whether you prefer the severance of relations between us.

"SINCERELY: LENIN, MARCH 5, 1923

(Commotion in the hall.)

Comrades! I will not comment on these documents. They speak eloquently for themselves. Since Stalin could behave in this manner during Lenin's life, could thus behave toward Nadezhda Konstantinovna Krupskaya – whom the Party knows well and values highly as a loyal friend of Lenin and as an active fighter for the cause of the Party since its creation – we can easily imagine how Stalin treated other people. These negative characteristics of his developed steadily and during the last years acquired an absolutely insufferable character.

As later events have proven, Lenin's anxiety was justified. In the first period after Lenin's death, Stalin still paid attention to his advice, but later he began to disregard the serious admonitions of Vladimir Ilyich. When we analyze the practice of Stalin in regard to the direction of the Party and of the country, when we pause to consider everything which Stalin perpetrated, we must be convinced that Lenin's fears were justified. The negative characteristics of Stalin, which, in Lenin's time, were only incipient, transformed themselves during the last years into a grave abuse of power by Stalin, which caused untold harm to our Party.

We have to consider seriously and analyze correctly this matter in order that we may preclude any possibility of a repetition in any form whatever of what took place during the life of Stalin, who absolutely did not tolerate collegiality in leadership and in work, and who practiced brutal violence, not only toward everything which opposed him, but also toward that which seemed, to his capricious and despotic character, contrary to his concepts.

Stalin acted not through persuasion, explanation and patient cooperation with people, but by imposing his concepts and demanding absolute submission to his opinion. Whoever opposed these concepts or tried to prove his [own] viewpoint and the correctness of his [own] position was doomed to removal from the leadership collective and to subsequent moral and physical annihilation. This was especially true during the period following the 17th Party Congress, when many prominent Party leaders and rank-and-file Party workers, honest and dedicated to the cause of Communism, fell victim to Stalin's despotism.

We must affirm that the Party fought a serious fight against the Trotskyites, rightists and bourgeois nationalists, and that it disarmed ideologically all the enemies of Leninism. This ideological fight was carried on successfully, as a result of which the Party became strengthened and tempered. Here Stalin played a positive role.

The Party led a great political-ideological struggle against those in its own ranks who proposed anti-Leninist theses, who represented a political line hostile to the Party and to the cause of socialism. This was a stubborn and a difficult fight but a necessary one, because the political line of both the Trotskyite-Zinovievite bloc and of the Bukharinites led actually toward the restoration of capitalism and toward capitulation to the world bourgeoisie. Let us consider for a moment what would have happened if in 1928-1929 the political line of right deviation had prevailed among us, or orientation toward "cotton-dress industrialization," or toward the kulak, etc. We would not now have a powerful heavy industry; we would not have the kolkhozes; we would find ourselves disarmed and weak in a capitalist encirclement.

It was for this reason that the Party led an inexorable ideological fight, explaining to all [its] members and to the non-Party masses the harm and the danger of the anti-Leninist proposals of the Trotskyite opposition and the rightist opportunists. And this great work of explaining the Party line bore fruit. Both the Trotskyites and the rightist opportunists were politically isolated. An overwhelming Party majority supported the Leninist line, and the Party was able to awaken and organize the working masses to apply the Leninist line and to build socialism.

A fact worth noting is that extreme repressive measures were not used against the Trotskyites, the Zinovievites, the Bukharinites, and others during the course of the furious ideological fight against them. The fight [in the 1920s] was on ideological grounds. But some years later, when socialism in our country was fundamentally constructed, when the exploiting classes were generally liquidated, when Soviet social structure had radically changed, when the social basis for political movements and groups hostile to the Party had violently contracted, when the ideological opponents of the Party were long since defeated politically – then repression directed against them began. It was precisely during this period (1935-1937-1938) that the practice of mass repression through the Government apparatus was born, first against the enemies of Leninism – Trotskyites, Zinovievites, Bukharinites, long since politically defeated by the Party – and subsequently also against many honest Communists, against those Party cadres who had borne the heavy load of the Civil War and the first and most difficult years of industrialization and collectivization, who had fought actively against the Trotskyites and the rightists for the Leninist Party line.

Stalin originated the concept "enemy of the people." This term automatically made it unnecessary that the ideological errors of a man or men engaged in a controversy be proven. It made possible the use of the cruelest repression, violating all norms of revolutionary legality, against anyone who in any way disagreed with Stalin, against those who were only suspected of hostile intent, against those who had bad reputations. The concept "enemy of the people" actually eliminated the possibility of any kind of ideological fight or the making of one's views known on this or that issue, even [issues] of a practical nature. On the whole, the only proof of guilt actually used, against all norms of current legal science, was the "confession" of the accused himself. As subsequent probing has proven, "confessions" were acquired through physical pressures against the accused. This led to glaring violations of revolutionary legality and to the fact that many entirely innocent individuals – [persons] who in the past had defended the Party line – became victims.

We must assert that, in regard to those persons who in their time had opposed the Party line, there were often no sufficiently serious reasons for their physical annihilation. The formula "enemy of the people" was specifically introduced for the purpose of physically annihilating such individuals.

It is a fact that many persons who were later annihilated as enemies of the Party and people had worked with Lenin during his life. Some of these persons had made errors during Lenin's life, but, despite this, Lenin benefited by their work; he corrected them and he did everything possible to retain them in the ranks of the Party; he induced them to follow him.

In this connection the delegates to the Party Congress should familiarize themselves with an unpublished note by V. I. Lenin directed to the Central Committee's Politburo in October

1920. Outlining the duties of the [Party] Control Commission, Lenin wrote that the Commission should be transformed into a real "organ of Party and proletarian conscience."

> "As a special duty of the Control Commission there is recommended a deep, individualized relationship with, and sometimes even a type of therapy for, the representatives of the so-called opposition – those who have experienced a psychological crisis because of failure in their Soviet or Party career. An effort should be made to quiet them, to explain the matter to them in a way used among comrades, to find for them (avoiding the method of issuing orders) a task for which they are psychologically fitted. Advice and rules relating to this matter are to be formulated by the Central Committee's Organizational Bureau, etc."

Everyone knows how irreconcilable Lenin was with the ideological enemies of Marxism, with those who deviated from the correct Party line. At the same time, however, Lenin, as is evident from the given document, in his practice of directing the Party demanded the most intimate Party contact with people who had shown indecision or temporary non-conformity with the Party line, but whom it was possible to return to the Party path. Lenin advised that such people should be patiently educated without the application of extreme methods.

Lenin's wisdom in dealing with people was evident in his work with cadres.

An entirely different relationship with people characterized Stalin. Lenin's traits – patient work with people, stubborn and painstaking education of them, the ability to induce people to follow him without using compulsion, but rather through the ideological influence on them of the whole collective – were entirely foreign to Stalin. He discarded the Leninist method of convincing and educating, he abandoned the method of ideological struggle for that of administrative violence, mass repressions and terror. He acted on an increasingly larger scale and more stubbornly through punitive organs, at the same time often violating all existing norms of morality and of Soviet laws.

Arbitrary behavior by one person encouraged and permitted arbitrariness in others. Mass arrests and deportations of many thousands of people, execution without trial and without normal investigation created conditions of insecurity, fear and even desperation.

This, of course, did not contribute toward unity of the Party ranks and of all strata of working people, but, on the contrary, brought about annihilation and the expulsion from the Party of workers who were loyal but inconvenient to Stalin.

Our Party fought for the implementation of Lenin's plans for the construction of socialism. This was an ideological fight. Had Leninist principles been observed during the course of this fight, had the Party's devotion to principles been skillfully combined with a keen and solicitous concern for people, had they not been repelled and wasted but rather drawn to our side, we certainly would not have had such a brutal violation of revolutionary legality and many thousands of people would not have fallen victim to the method of terror. Extraordinary methods would then have been resorted to only against those people who had in fact committed criminal acts against the Soviet system.

Let us recall some historical facts.

In the days before the October Revolution, two members of the Central Committee of the Bolshevik Party – Kamenev and Zinoviev – declared themselves against Lenin's plan for an armed uprising. In addition, on October 18 they published in the Menshevik newspaper, *Novaya Zhizn*, a statement declaring that the Bolsheviks were making preparations for an uprising and that they considered it adventuristic. Kamenev and Zinoviev thus disclosed to the enemy the decision of the Central Committee to stage the uprising, and that the uprising had been organized to take place within the very near future.

This was treason against the Party and against the Revolution. In this connection, V. I. Lenin wrote: "Kamenev and Zinoviev revealed the decision of the Central Committee of their Party on the armed uprising to [Mikhail] Rodzyanko and [Alexander] Kerensky.... He put before the Central Committee the question of Zinoviev's and Kamenev's expulsion from the Party.

However, after the Great Socialist October Revolution, as is known, Zinoviev and Kamenev were given leading positions. Lenin put them in positions in which they carried out most responsible Party tasks and participated actively in the work of the leading Party and Soviet organs. It is known that Zinoviev and Kamenev committed a number of other serious errors during Lenin's life. In his "Testament" Lenin warned that "Zinoviev's and Kamenev's October episode was of course not an accident." But Lenin did not pose the question of their arrest and certainly not their shooting.

Or, let us take the example of the Trotskyites. At present, after a sufficiently long historical period, we can speak about the fight with the Trotskyites with complete calm and can analyze this matter with sufficient objectivity. After all, around Trotsky were people whose origin cannot by any means be traced to bourgeois society. Part of them belonged to the Party intelligentsia and a certain part were recruited from among the workers. We can name many individuals who, in their time, joined the Trotskyites; however, these same individuals took an active part in the workers' movement before the Revolution, during the Socialist October Revolution itself, and also in the consolidation of the victory of this greatest of revolutions. Many of them broke with Trotskyism and returned to Leninist positions. Was it necessary to annihilate such people? We are deeply convinced that, had Lenin lived, such an extreme method would not have been used against any of them.

Such are only a few historical facts. But can it be said that Lenin did not decide to use even the most severe means against enemies of the Revolution when this was actually necessary? No; no one can say this. Vladimir Ilyich demanded uncompromising dealings with the enemies of the Revolution and of the working class and when necessary resorted ruthlessly to such methods. You will recall only V. I. Lenin's fight with the Socialist Revolutionary organizers of the anti-Soviet uprising, with the counterrevolutionary kulaks in 1918 and with others, when Lenin without hesitation used the most extreme methods against the enemies. Lenin used such methods, however, only against actual class enemies and not against those who blunder, who err, and whom it was possible to lead through ideological influence and even retain in the leadership. Lenin used severe methods only in the most necessary cases, when the exploiting classes were still in existence and were vigorously opposing the Revolution, when the struggle for survival was decidedly assuming the sharpest forms, even including a Civil War.

Stalin, on the other hand, used extreme methods and mass repressions at a time when the Revolution was already victorious, when the Soviet state was strengthened, when the exploiting classes were already liquidated and socialist relations were rooted solidly in all phases of national economy, when our Party was politically consolidated and had strengthened itself both numerically and ideologically.

It is clear that here Stalin showed in a whole series of cases his intolerance, his brutality and his abuse of power. Instead of proving his political correctness and mobilizing the masses, he often chose the path of repression and physical annihilation, not only against actual enemies, but also against individuals who had not committed any crimes against the Party and the Soviet Government. Here we see no wisdom but only a demonstration of the brutal force which had once so alarmed V. I. Lenin.

Lately, especially after the unmasking of the Beria gang, the Central Committee looked into a series of matters fabricated by this gang. This revealed a very ugly picture of brutal willfulness connected with the incorrect behavior of Stalin. As facts prove, Stalin, using his unlimited power, allowed himself many abuses, acting in the name of the Central Committee, not asking for the opinion of the Committee members nor even of the members of the Central Committee's Politburo; often he did not inform them about his personal decisions concerning very important Party and government matters.

Considering the question of the cult of an individual, we must first of all show everyone what harm this caused to the interests of our Party.

Vladimir Ilyich Lenin had always stressed the Party's role and significance in the direction of the socialist government of workers and peasants; he saw in this the chief precondition for a successful building of socialism in our country. Pointing to the great responsibility of the Bolshevik Party, as ruling Party of the Soviet state, Lenin called for the most meticulous observance of all norms of Party life; he called for the realization of the principles of collegiality in the direction of the Party and the state.

Collegiality of leadership flows from the very nature of our Party, a Party built on the principles of democratic centralism. "This means," said Lenin, "that all Party matters are accomplished by all Party members – directly or through representatives – who, without any exceptions, are subject to the same rules; in addition, all administrative members, all directing collegia, all holders of Party positions are elective, they must account for their activities and are recallable."

It is known that Lenin himself offered an example of the most careful observance of these principles. There was no matter so important that Lenin himself decided it without asking for advice and approval of the majority of the Central Committee members or of the members of the Central Committee's Politburo. In the most difficult period for our Party and our country, Lenin considered it necessary regularly to convoke Congresses, Party Conferences and Plenary sessions of the Central Committee at which all the most important questions were discussed and where resolutions, carefully worked out by the collective of leaders, were approved.

We can recall, for an example, the year 1918 when the country was threatened by the attack of the imperialistic interventionists. In this situation the 7th Party Congress was convened in order to discuss a vitally important matter which could not be postponed – the matter of peace. In 1919, while the Civil

War was raging, the 8th Party Congress convened which adopted a new Party program, decided such important matters as the relationship with the peasant masses, the organization of the Red Army, the leading role of the Party in the work of the soviets, the correction of the social composition of the Party, and other matters. In 1920 the 9th Party Congress was convened which laid down guiding principles pertaining to the Party's work in the sphere of economic construction. In 1921 the 10th Party Congress accepted Lenin's New Economic Policy and the historic resolution called "On Party Unity."

During Lenin's life, Party congresses were convened regularly; always, when a radical turn in the development of the Party and the country took place, Lenin considered it absolutely necessary that the Party discuss at length all the basic matters pertaining to internal and foreign policy and to questions bearing on the development of Party and government.

It is very characteristic that Lenin addressed to the Party Congress as the highest Party organ his last articles, letters and remarks. During the period between congresses, the Central Committee of the Party, acting as the most authoritative leading collective, meticulously observed the principles of the Party and carried out its policy.

So it was during Lenin's life. Were our Party's holy Leninist principles observed after the death of Vladimir Ilyich?

Whereas, during the first few years after Lenin's death,

Party Congresses and Central Committee Plenums took place more or less regularly, later, when Stalin began increasingly to abuse his power, these principles were brutally violated. This was especially evident during the last 15 years of his life. Was it a normal situation when over 13 years elapsed between the 18th and 19th Party Congresses, years during which our Party and our country had experienced so many important events? These events demanded categorically that the Party should have passed resolutions pertaining to the country's defense during the [Great] Patriotic War and to peacetime construction after the war.

Even after the end of the war a Congress was not convened for over seven years. Central Committee Plenums were hardly ever called. It should be sufficient to mention that during all the years of the Patriotic War not a single Central Committee Plenum took place. It is true that there was an attempt to call a Central Committee Plenum in October 1941, when Central Committee members from the whole country were called to Moscow. They waited two days for the opening of the Plenum, but in vain. Stalin did not even want to meet and talk to the Central Committee members. This fact shows how demoralized Stalin was in the first months of the war and how haughtily and disdainfully he treated the Central Committee members.

In practice, Stalin ignored the norms of Party life and trampled on the Leninist principle of collective Party leadership.

Stalin's willfulness vis a vis the Party and its Central

Committee became fully evident after the 17th Party Congress, which took place in 1934.

Having at its disposal numerous data showing brutal willfulness toward Party cadres, the Central Committee has created a Party commission under the control of the Central Committee's Presidium. It has been charged with investigating what made possible mass repressions against the majority of the Central Committee members and candidates elected at the 17th Congress of the All-Union Communist Party (Bolsheviks).

The commission has become acquainted with a large quantity of materials in the NKVD archives and with other documents. It has established many facts pertaining to the fabrication of cases against Communists, to false accusations, [and] to glaring abuses of socialist legality, which resulted in the death of innocent people. It became apparent that many Party, Soviet and economic activists who in 1937-1938 were branded "enemies" were actually never enemies, spies, wreckers, etc., but were always honest Communists. They were merely stigmatized [as enemies]. Often, no longer able to bear barbaric tortures, they charged themselves (at the order of the investigative judges/falsifiers) with all kinds of grave and unlikely crimes.

The commission has presented to the Central Committee's Presidium lengthy and documented materials pertaining to mass repressions against the delegates to the 17th Party Congress and against members of the Central Committee elected at that

Congress. These materials have been studied by the Presidium..

It was determined that of the 139 members and candidates of the Central Committee who were elected at the 17th Congress, 98 persons, i.e., 70 per cent, were arrested and shot (mostly in 1937-1938). (Indignation in the hall.) What was the composition of the delegates to the 17th Congress? It is known that 80 per cent of the voting participants of the 17th Congress joined the Party during the years of conspiracy before the Revolution and during the Civil War, i.e. meaning before 1921. By social origin the basic mass of the delegates to the Congress were workers (60 per cent of the voting members).

For this reason, it is inconceivable that a Congress so composed could have elected a Central Committee in which a majority [of the members] would prove to be enemies of the Party. The only reasons why 70 per cent of the Central Committee members and candidates elected at the 17th Congress were branded as enemies of the Party and of the people were because honest Communists were slandered, accusations against them were fabricated, and revolutionary legality was gravely undermined.

The same fate met not only Central Committee members but also the majority of the delegates to the 17th Party Congress. Of 1,966 delegates with either voting or advisory rights, 1,108 persons were arrested on charges of anti-revolutionary crimes, i.e., decidedly more than a majority. This very fact shows how absurd, wild and contrary to common sense were the charges of counterrevolutionary crimes made out, as we now see, against a majority of participants at the 17th Party Congress.

(Indignation in the hall.)

We should recall that the 17th Party Congress is known historically as the Congress of Victors. Delegates to the Congress were active participants in the building of our socialist state; many of them suffered and fought for Party interests during the pre-Revolutionary years in the conspiracy and at the civil-war fronts; they fought their enemies valiantly and often nervelessly looked into the face of death.

How, then, can we believe that such people could prove to be "two-faced" and had joined the camps of the enemies of socialism during the era after the political liquidation of Zinovievites, Trotskyites and rightists and after the great accomplishments of socialist construction? This was the result of the abuse of power by Stalin, who began to use mass terror against Party cadres.

What is the reason that mass repressions against activists increased more and more after the 17th Party Congress? It was because at that time Stalin had so elevated himself above the Party and above the nation that he ceased to consider either the Central Committee or the Party.

Stalin still reckoned with the opinion of the collective before the 17th Congress. After the complete political liquidation of the

Trotskyites, Zinovievites and Bukharinites, however, when the Party had achieved unity, Stalin to an ever greater degree stopped considering the members of the Party's Central Committee and even the members of the Politburo. Stalin thought that now he could decide all things alone and that all he needed were statisticians. He treated all others in such a way that they could only listen to him and praise him.

After the criminal murder of Sergey M. Kirov, mass repressions and brutal acts of violation of socialist legality began. On the evening of December 1, 1934 on Stalin's initiative (without the approval of the Politburo –which was given two days later, casually), the Secretary of the Presidium of the Central Executive Committee, [Abel] Yenukidze, signed the following directive:

"1. Investigative agencies are directed to speed up the cases of those accused of the preparation or execution of acts of terror.

"2. Judicial organs are directed not to hold up the execution of death sentences pertaining to crimes of this category in order to consider the possibility of pardon, because the Presidium of the Central Executive Committee of the USSR does not consider as possible the receiving of petitions of this sort.

"3. The organs of the Commissariat of Internal Affairs [NKVD] are directed to execute the death sentences against criminals of the above-mentioned category immediately after the passage of sentences."

This directive became the basis for mass acts of abuse against socialist legality. During many of the fabricated court cases, the accused were charged with "the preparation" of terroristic acts; this deprived them of any possibility that their cases might be re-examined, even when they stated before the court that their "confessions" were secured by force, and when, in a convincing manner, they disproved the accusations against them.

It must be asserted that to this day the circumstances surrounding Kirov's murder hide many things which are inexplicable and mysterious and demand a most careful examination. There are reasons for the suspicion that the killer of Kirov, [Leonid] Nikolayev, was assisted by someone from among the people whose duty it was to protect the person of Kirov.

A month and a half before the killing, Nikolayev was arrested on the grounds of suspicious behavior but he was released and not even searched. It is an unusually suspicious circumstance that when the Chekist assigned to protect Kirov was being brought for an interrogation, on December 2, 1934, he was killed in a car "accident" in which no other occupants of the car were harmed. After the murder of Kirov, top functionaries of the Leningrad NKVD were given very light sentences, but in 1937 they were shot. We can assume that they were shot in order to cover up the traces of the organizers of Kirov's killing.

(Movement in the hall.)

Mass repressions grew tremendously from the end of 1936 after a telegram from Stalin and [Andrey] Zhdanov, dated from Sochi on September 25, 1936, was addressed to [Lazar] Kaganovich, [Vyacheslav] Molotov and other members of the Politburo. The content of the telegram was as follows:

"We deem it absolutely necessary and urgent that comrade [Nikolay] Yezhov be nominated to the post of People's Commissar for Internal Affairs. [Genrikh] Yagoda definitely has proven himself incapable of unmasking the Trotskyite-Zinovievite bloc. The OGPU is four years behind in this matter. This is noted by all Party workers and by the majority of the representatives of the NKVD."

Strictly speaking, we should stress that Stalin did not meet with and, therefore, could not know the opinion of Party workers.

This Stalinist formulation that the "NKVD is four years behind" in applying mass repression and that there is a necessity for "catching up" with the neglected work directly pushed the NKVD workers on the path of mass arrests and executions.

We should state that this formulation was also forced on the February-March Plenary session of the Central Committee of the

All-Union Communist Party (Bolsheviks) in 1937. The Plenary resolution approved it on the basis of Yezhov's report, "Lessons flowing from the harmful activity, diversion and espionage of the Japanese-German-Trotskyite agents," stating:

> "The Plenum of the Central Committee of the All-Union Communist Party (Bolsheviks) considers that all facts revealed during the investigation into the matter of an anti-Soviet Trotskyite center and of its followers in the provinces show that the People's Commissariat of Internal Affairs has fallen behind at least four years in the attempt to unmask these most inexorable enemies of the people."

The mass repressions at this time were made under the slogan of a fight against the Trotskyites. Did the Trotskyites at this time actually constitute such a danger to our Party and to the Soviet state? We should recall that in 1927, on the eve of the 15th Party Congress, only some 4,000 [Party] votes were cast for the Trotskyite-Zinovievite opposition while there were 724,000 for the Party line. During the 10 years which passed between the 15th Party Congress and the February-March Central Committee Plenum, Trotskyism was completely disarmed. Many former Trotskyites changed their former views and worked in the various sectors building socialism. It is clear that in the situation of socialist victory there was no basis for mass terror in the country.

Stalin's report at the February-March Central Committee Plenum in 1937, "Deficiencies of Party work and methods for the liquidation of the Trotskyites and of other two-facers," contained an attempt at theoretical justification of the mass terror policy under the pretext that class war must allegedly sharpen as we march forward toward socialism. Stalin asserted that both history and Lenin taught him this.

Actually Lenin taught that the application of revolutionary violence is necessitated by the resistance of the exploiting classes, and this referred to the era when the exploiting classes existed and were powerful. As soon as the nation's political situation had improved, when in January 1920 the Red Army took Rostov and thus won a most important victory over [General A. I.] Denikin, Lenin instructed [Felix] Dzerzhinsky to stop mass terror and to abolish the death penalty. Lenin justified this important political move of the Soviet state in the following manner in his report at the session of the All-Union Central Executive Committee on February 2, 1920:

"We were forced to use terror because of the terror practiced by the Entente, when strong world powers threw their hordes against us, not avoiding any type of conduct. We would not have lasted two days had we not answered these attempts of officers and White Guardists in a merciless fashion; this meant the use of terror, but this was forced upon us by the terrorist methods of the Entente.

"But as soon as we attained a decisive victory, even before the end of the war, immediately after taking Rostov, we gave up the use of the death penalty and thus proved that we intend to execute our own program in the manner that we promised. We say that the application of violence flows out of the decision to smother the exploiters, the big landowners and the capitalists; as soon as this was accomplished we gave up the use of all extraordinary methods. We have proved this in practice."

Stalin deviated from these clear and plain precepts of Lenin. Stalin put the Party and the NKVD up to the use of mass terror when the exploiting classes had been liquidated in our country and when there were no serious reasons for the use of extraordinary mass terror.

This terror was actually directed not at the remnants of the defeated exploiting classes but against the honest workers of the Party and of the Soviet state; against them were made lying, slanderous and absurd accusations concerning "two-facedness," "espionage," "sabotage," preparation of fictitious "plots," etc.

At the February-March Central Committee Plenum in 1937 many members actually questioned the rightness of the established course regarding mass repressions under the pretext of combating "two-facedness."

Comrade [Pavel] Postyshev most ably expressed these doubts. He said:

"I have philosophized that the severe years of fighting have passed. Party members who have lost their backbones have broken down or have joined the camp of the enemy; healthy elements have fought for the Party. These were the years of industrialization and collectivization. I never thought it possible that after this severe era had passed Karpov and people like him would find themselves in the camp of the enemy. Karpov was a worker in the Ukrainian Central Committee whom Postyshev knew well.) And now, according to the testimony, it appears that Karpov was recruited in 1934 by the Trotskyites. I personally do not believe that in 1934 an honest Party member who had trod the long road of unrelenting fight against enemies for the Party and for socialism would now be in the camp of the enemies. I do not believe it.... I cannot imagine how it would be possible to travel with the Party during the difficult years and then, in 1934, join the Trotskyites. It is an odd thing...."

(Movement in the hall.)

Using Stalin's formulation, namely, that the closer we are to socialism the more enemies we will have, and using the resolution of the February-March Central Committee Plenum passed on the basis of Yezhov's report, the provocateurs who had infiltrated the state-security organs together with conscienceless careerists began to protect with the Party name the mass terror against Party cadres, cadres of the Soviet state, and ordinary Soviet citizens. It should suffice to say that the number of arrests based on charges of counterrevolutionary crimes had grown ten times between 1936 and 1937.

It is known that brutal willfulness was practiced against leading Party workers. The [relevant] Party statute, approved at the 17th Party Congress, was based on Leninist principles expressed at the 10th Party Congress. It stated that, in order to apply an extreme method such as exclusion from the Party against a Central Committee member, against a Central Committee candidate or against a member of the Party Control Commission, "it is necessary to call a Central Committee Plenum and to invite to the Plenum all Central Committee candidate members and all members of the Party Control Commission"; only if two-thirds of the members of such a general assembly of responsible Party leaders found it necessary, only then could a Central Committee member or candidate be expelled.

The majority of those Central Committee's members and candidates who were elected at the 17th Congress and arrested in 1937-1938 were expelled from the Party illegally through brutal abuse of the Party statute, because the question of their expulsion was never studied at the Central Committee Plenum.

Now, when the cases of some of these so-called "spies" and "saboteurs" were examined, it was found that all their cases were fabricated. The confessions of guilt of many of those arrested and charged with enemy activity were gained with the help of cruel and inhuman tortures.

At the same time, Stalin, as we have been informed by members of the Politburo of that time, did not show them the statements of many accused political activists when they retracted their confessions before the military tribunal and asked for an objective examination of their cases. There were many such declarations, and Stalin doubtless knew of them.

The Central Committee considers it absolutely necessary to inform the Congress of many such fabricated "cases" against the members of the Party's Central Committee elected at the 17th Party Congress.

An example of vile provocation, of odious falsification and of criminal violation of revolutionary legality is the case of the former candidate for the Central Committee Politburo, one of the most eminent workers of the Party and of the Soviet Government, comrade [Robert] Eikhe, who had been a Party member since 1905.

(Commotion in the hall.)

Comrade Eikhe was arrested on April 29, 1938 on the basis of slanderous materials, without the sanction of the [State]

Prosecutor of the USSR. This was finally received 15 months after the arrest.

The investigation of Eikhe's case was made in a manner which most brutally violated Soviet legality and was accompanied by willfulness and falsification.

Under torture, Eikhe was forced to sign a protocol of his confession prepared in advance by the investigative judges. In it, he and several other eminent Party workers were accused of anti-Soviet activity.

On October 1, 1939 Eikhe sent his declaration to Stalin in which he categorically denied his guilt and asked for an examination of his case. In the declaration he wrote: "There is no more bitter misery than to sit in the jail of a government for which I have always fought."

A second declaration of Eikhe has been preserved, which he sent to Stalin on October 27, 1939. In it [Eikhe] cited facts very convincingly and countered the slanderous accusations made against him, arguing that this provocatory accusation was on one hand the work of real Trotskyites whose arrests he had sanctioned as First Secretary of the West Siberian Regional Party Committee and who conspired in order to take revenge on him, and, on the other hand, the result of the base falsification of materials by the investigative judges.

Eikhe wrote in his declaration:

"... On October 25 of this year I was informed that the investigation in my case has been concluded and I was given access to the materials of this investigation. Had I been guilty of only one hundredth of the crimes with which I am charged, I would not have dared to send you this pre-execution declaration. However I have not been guilty of even one of the things with which I am charged and my heart is clean of even the shadow of baseness. I have never in my life told you a word of falsehood, and now, finding both feet in the grave, I am still not lying. My whole case is a typical example of provocation, slander and violation of the elementary basis of revolutionary legality....

"... The confessions which were made part of my file are not only absurd but contain slander toward the Central Committee of the All-Union Communist Party (Bolsheviks) and toward the Council of People's Commissars. [This is] because correct resolutions of the Central Committee of the All-Union Communist Party (Bolsheviks) and of the Council of People's Commissars which were not made on my initiative and [were promulgated] without my participation are presented as hostile acts of counterrevolutionary organizations made at my suggestion.

"I am now alluding to the most disgraceful part of my life and to my really grave guilt against the Party and against you. This is my confession of counterrevolutionary activity.... The case is as follows: Not being able to suffer the tortures to which I was submitted by [Z.] Ushakov and Nikolayev – especially by the former, who utilized the knowledge that my broken ribs have not properly mended and have caused me great pain – I have been forced to accuse myself and others.

"The majority of my confession has been suggested or dictated by Ushakov. The rest is my reconstruction of NKVD materials from Western Siberia for which I assumed all responsibility. If some part of the story which Ushakov fabricated and which I signed did not properly hang together, I was forced to sign another variation. The same thing was done to [Moisey] Rukhimovich, who was at first designated as a member of the reserve net and whose name later was removed without telling me anything about it. The same also was done with the leader of the reserve net, supposedly created by Bukharin in 1935. At first I wrote my [own] name in, and then I was instructed to insert [Valery] Mezhlauk's. There were other similar incidents.

"... I am asking and begging you that you again examine my case, and this not for the purpose of sparing me but in order to unmask the vile provocation which, like a snake, wound itself around many persons in a great degree due to my meanness and criminal slander. I have never betrayed you or the Party. I know that I perish because of vile and mean work of enemies of the Party and of the people, who have fabricated the provocation against me."

It would appear that such an important declaration was worth an examination by the Central Committee. This, however, was not done. The declaration was transmitted to Beria while the terrible maltreatment of the Politburo candidate, comrade Eikhe, continued.

On February 2, 1940, Eikhe was brought before the court. Here he did not confess any guilt and said as follows:

"In all the so-called confessions of mine there is not one letter written by me with the exception of my signatures under the protocols, which were forced from me. I have made my confession under pressure from the investigative judge, who from the time of my arrest tormented me. After that I began to write all this nonsense.... The most important thing for me is to tell the court, the Party and Stalin that I am not guilty. I have never been guilty of any conspiracy. I will die believing in the truth of Party policy as I have believed in it during my whole life."

On February 4, Eikhe was shot.

(Indignation in the hall.)

It has been definitely established now that Eikhe's case was fabricated. He has been rehabilitated posthumously.

Comrade [Yan] Rudzutak, a candidate-member of the

Politburo, a member of the Party since 1905 who spent 10 years in a Tsarist hard-labor camp, completely retracted in court the confession forced from him. The protocol of the session of the Collegium of the Supreme Military Court contains the following statement by Rudzutak:

"... The only plea which [the defendant] places before the court is that the Central Committee of the All-Union Communist Party (Bolsheviks) be informed that there is in the NKVD an as yet not liquidated center which is craftily manufacturing cases, which forces innocent persons to confess. There is no opportunity to prove one's non-participation in crimes to which the confessions of various persons testify. The investigative methods are such that they force people to lie and to slander entirely innocent persons in addition to those who already stand accused. [The defendant] asks the Court that he be allowed to inform the Central Committee of the All-Union Communist Party (Bolsheviks) about all this in writing. He assures the Court that he personally had never any evil designs in regard to the policy of our Party because he has always agreed with Party policy concerning all spheres of economic and cultural activity."

This declaration of Rudzutak was ignored, despite the fact

that Rudzutak was in his time the head of the Central Control Commission– which had been called into being, in accordance with Lenin's conception, for the purpose of fighting for Party unity. In this manner fell the head of this highly authoritative Party organ, a victim of brutal willfulness. He was not even called before the Politburo because Stalin did not want to talk to him. Sentence was pronounced on him in 20 minutes and he was shot.

(Indignation in the hall.)

After careful examination of the case in 1955, it was established that the accusation against Rudzutak was false and that it was based on slanderous materials. Rudzutak has been rehabilitated posthumously.

The way in which the former NKVD workers manufactured various fictitious "anti-Soviet centers" and "blocs" with the help of provocatory methods is seen from the confession of comrade Rozenblum, a Party member since 1906, who was arrested in 1937 by the Leningrad NKVD.

During the examination in 1955 of the Komarov case, Rozenblum revealed the following fact: When Rozenblum was arrested in 1937, he was subjected to terrible torture during which he was ordered to confess false information concerning himself and other persons. He was then brought to the office of [Leonid] Zakovsky, who offered him freedom on condition that he make before the court a false confession fabricated in 1937 by the NKVD concerning "sabotage, espionage and diversion in a terroristic center in Leningrad." (Movement in the hall.) With unbelievable cynicism, Zakovsky told about the vile "mechanism" for the crafty creation of fabricated "anti-Soviet plots."

"In order to illustrate it to me," stated Rozenblum, "Zakovsky gave me several possible variants of the organization of this center and of its branches. After he detailed the organization to me, Zakovsky told me that the NKVD would prepare the case of this center, remarking that the trial would be public. Before the court were to be brought 4 or 5 members of this center: [Mikhail] Chudov, [Fyodor] Ugarov, [Pyotr] Smorodin, [Boris] Pozern, Chudov's wife [Liudmilla] Shaposhnikova and others together with 2 or 3 members from the branches of this center....

"... The case of the Leningrad center has to be built solidly, and for this reason witnesses are needed. Social origin (of course, in the past) and the Party standing of the witness will play more than a small role. "'You, yourself,' said Zakovsky, 'will not need to invent anything. The NKVD will prepare for you a ready outline for every branch of the center. You will have to study it carefully, and remember well all questions the Court might ask and their answers. This case will be ready in four or five months, perhaps in half a year. During all this time you will be preparing yourself so that you will not compromise the investigation and yourself. Your future will depend on how the trial goes and on its results. If you begin to lie and to testify falsely, blame yourself. If you manage to endure it, you will save your head and we will feed and clothe you at the Government's cost until your death.'"

This is the kind of vile thing practiced then.

(Movement in the hall.)

Even more widely was the falsification of cases practiced in the provinces. The NKVD headquarters of the Sverdlov Province "discovered" a so-called "Ural uprising staff" – an organ of the bloc of rightists, Trotskyites, Socialist Revolutionaries, and church leaders – whose chief supposedly was the Secretary of the Sverdlov Provincial Party Committee and member of the Central Committee, All-Union Communist Party (Bolsheviks), [Ivan] Kabakov, who had been a Party member since 1914. Investigative materials of that time show that in almost all regions, provinces and republics there supposedly existed "rightist Trotskyite, espionage-terror and diversionary-sabotage organizations and centers" and that the heads of such organizations as a rule – for no known reason – were First Secretaries of provincial or republican Communist Party committees or Central Committees.

Many thousands of honest and innocent Communists have died as a result of this monstrous falsification of such "cases," as a result of the fact that all kinds of slanderous "confessions" were accepted, and as a result of the practice of forcing accusations against oneself and others. In the same manner were fabricated the "cases" against eminent Party and state workers – [Stanislav] Kosior, [Vlas] Chubar, [Pavel] Postyshev, [Alexander] Kosarev, and others.

In those years repressions on a mass scale were applied which were based on nothing tangible and which resulted in heavy cadre losses to the Party.

The vicious practice was condoned of having the NKVD prepare lists of persons whose cases were under the jurisdiction of the Military Collegium and whose sentences were prepared in advance. Yezhov would send these [execution] lists to Stalin personally for his approval of the proposed punishment. In 1937-1938, 383 such lists containing the names of many thousands of Party, Soviet, Komsomol, Army, and economic workers were sent to Stalin. He approved these lists.

A large part of these cases are being reviewed now. A great many are being voided because they were baseless and falsified. Suffice it to say that from 1954 to the present time the Military Collegium of the Supreme Court has rehabilitated 7,679 persons, many of whom have been rehabilitated posthumously.

Mass arrests of Party, Soviet, economic and military workers caused tremendous harm to our country and to the cause of socialist advancement.

Mass repressions had a negative influence on the moral-political condition of the Party, created a situation of uncertainty, contributed to the spreading of unhealthy suspicion, and sowed distrust among Communists. All sorts of slanderers and careerists were active.

Resolutions of the January, 1938 Central Committee Plenum brought some measure of improvement to Party organizations. However, widespread repression also existed in 1938.

Only because our Party has at its disposal such great moral-political strength was it possible for it to survive the difficult events in 1937-1938 and to educate new cadres. There is, however, no doubt that our march forward toward socialism and toward the preparation of the country's defense would have been much more successful were it not for the tremendous loss in the cadres suffered as a result of the baseless and false mass repressions in 1937-1938.

We are accusing Yezhov justly for the degenerate practices of 1937. But we have to answer these questions: Could Yezhov have arrested Kosior, for instance, without Stalin's knowledge? Was there an exchange of opinions or a Politburo decision concerning this?

No, there was not, as there was none regarding other cases of this type. Could Yezhov have decided such important matters as the fate of such eminent Party figures?

No, it would be a display of naiveté to consider this the work of Yezhov alone. It is clear that these matters were decided by Stalin, and that without his orders and his sanction Yezhov could not have done this.

We have examined these cases and have rehabilitated Kosior, Rudzutak, Postyshev, Kosarev and others. For what causes were they arrested and sentenced? Our review of evidence shows that there was no reason for this. They, like many others, were arrested without prosecutorial knowledge.

In such a situation, there is no need for any sanction, for what sort of a sanction could there be when Stalin decided everything? He was the chief prosecutor in these cases. Stalin not only agreed to arrest orders but issued them on his own initiative. We must say this so that the delegates to the Congress can clearly undertake and themselves assess this and draw the proper conclusions.

Facts prove that many abuses were made on Stalin's orders without reckoning with any norms of Party and Soviet legality. Stalin was a very distrustful man, sickly suspicious. We know this from our work with him. He could look at a man and say: "Why are your eyes so shifty today?" or "Why are you turning so much today and avoiding to look me directly in the eyes?" The sickly suspicion created in him a general distrust even toward eminent Party workers whom he had known for years. Everywhere and in everything he saw "enemies," "two-facers" and "spies." Possessing unlimited power, he indulged in great willfulness and stifled people morally as well as physically. A situation was created where one could not express one's own volition.

When Stalin said that one or another should be arrested, it was necessary to accept on faith that he was an "enemy of the people." Meanwhile, Beria's gang, which ran the organs of state security, outdid itself in proving the guilt of the arrested and the truth of materials which it falsified. And what proofs were offered? The confessions of the arrested, and the investigative judges accepted these "confessions." And how is it possible that a person confesses to crimes which he has not committed? Only in one way –because of the application of physical methods of pressuring him, tortures, bringing him to a state of unconsciousness, deprivation of his judgment, taking away of his human dignity. In this manner were "confessions" acquired.

The wave of mass arrests began to recede in 1939. When the leaders of territorial Party organizations began to accuse NKVD workers of using methods of physical pressure on the arrested, Stalin dispatched a coded telegram on January 20, 1939 to the committee secretaries of provinces and regions, to the central committees of republican Communist parties, to the [republican] People's Commissars of Internal Affairs and to the heads of NKVD organizations. This telegram stated:

"The Central Committee of the All-Union Communist Party (Bolsheviks) explains that the application of methods of physical pressure in NKVD practice is permissible from 1937 on in accordance with permission of the Central Committee of the All-Union Communist Party (Bolsheviks) ... It is known that all bourgeois intelligence services use methods of physical influence against representatives of the socialist proletariat and that they use them in their most scandalous forms.

"The question arises as to why the socialist intelligence service should be more humanitarian against the mad agents of the bourgeoisie, against the deadly enemies of the working class and of kolkhoz workers. The Central Committee of the All-Union Communist Party (Bolsheviks) considers that physical pressure should still be used obligatorily, as an exception applicable to known and obstinate enemies of the people, as a method both justifiable and appropriate."

Thus, Stalin had sanctioned in the name of the Central Committee of the All-Union Communist Party (Bolsheviks) the most brutal violation of socialist legality, torture and oppression, which led as we have seen to the slandering and to the self-accusation of innocent people.

Not long ago – only several days before the present Congress – we called to the Central Committee Presidium session and interrogated the investigative judge Rodos, who in his time investigated and interrogated Kosior, Chubar and Kosarev. He is a vile person, with the brain of a bird, and completely degenerate morally. It was this man who was deciding the fate of prominent Party workers. He also was making judgments concerning the politics in these matters, because, having established their "crime," he thereby provided materials from which important political implications could be drawn.

The question arises whether a man with such an intellect could–by himelf–have conducted his investigations in a manner proving the guilt of people such as Kosior and others. No, he could not have done it without proper directives. At the Central Committee Presidium session he told us: "I was told that Kosior and Chubar were people's enemies and for this reason I, as an investigative judge, had to make them confess that they were enemies."

(Indignation in the hall.)

He would do this only through long tortures, which he did, receiving detailed instructions from Beria. We must say that at the Central Committee Presidium session he cynically declared: "I thought that I was executing the orders of the Party." In this manner, Stalin's orders concerning the use of methods of physical pressure against the arrested were carried out in practice.

These and many other facts show that all norms of correct Party solution of problems were [in]validated and that everything was dependent upon the willfulness of one man.

The power accumulated in the hands of one person, Stalin, led to serious consequences during the Great Patriotic War.

When we look at many of our novels, films and historical-scientific studies, the role of Stalin in the Patriotic War appears to be entirely improbable. Stalin had foreseen everything. The Soviet Army, on the basis of a strategic plan prepared by Stalin long before, used the tactics of so-called "active defense," i.e., tactics which, as we know, allowed the Germans to come up to Moscow and Stalingrad. Using such tactics, the Soviet Army, supposedly thanks only to Stalin's genius, turned to the offensive and subdued the enemy. The epic victory gained through the armed might of the land of the Soviets, through our heroic people, is ascribed in this type of novel, film and "scientific study" as being completely due to the strategic genius of Stalin.

We have to analyze this matter carefully because it has a tremendous significance not only from the historical, but especially from the political, educational and practical points of view. What are the facts of this matter?

Before the war, our press and all our political-educational work was characterized by its bragging tone: When an enemy violates the holy Soviet soil, then for every blow of the enemy we will answer with three, and we will battle the enemy on his soil and we will win without much harm to ourselves. But these positive statements were not based in all areas on concrete facts, which would actually guarantee the immunity of our borders.

During the war and after the war, Stalin advanced the thesis that the tragedy our nation experienced in the first part of the war was the result of an "unexpected" attack by the Germans against the Soviet Union. But, comrades, this is completely untrue. As soon as Hitler came to power in Germany he assigned to himself the task of liquidating Communism. The fascists were saying this openly. They did not hide their plans.

In order to attain this aggressive end, all sorts of pacts and blocs were created, such as the famous Berlin-Rome-Tokyo Axis. Many facts from the prewar period clearly showed that Hitler was going all out to begin a war against the Soviet state, and that he had concentrated large armies, together with armored units, near the Soviet borders.

Documents which have now been published show that [as early as] April 3, 1941 Churchill, through his ambassador to the USSR, [Sir Stafford] Cripps, personally warned Stalin that the Germans had begun regrouping their armed units with the intent of attacking the Soviet Union.

It is self-evident that Churchill did not do this at all because of his friendly feeling toward the Soviet nation. He had in this his own imperialistic goals – to bring Germany and the USSR into a bloody war and thereby to strengthen the position of the British Empire.

All the same, Churchill affirmed in his writings that he sought to "warn Stalin and call his attention to the danger which threatened him." Churchill stressed this repeatedly in his dispatches of April 18 and on the following days. However, Stalin took no heed of these warnings. What is more, Stalin ordered that no credence be given to information of this sort, so as not to provoke the initiation of military operations.

We must assert that information of this sort concerning the threat of German armed invasion of Soviet territory was coming in also from our own military and diplomatic sources. However, because the leadership was conditioned against such information, such data was dispatched with fear and assessed with reservation. Thus, for instance, information sent from Berlin on May 6, 1941 by the Soviet military (sic) attaché, Captain (sic) Vorontsov, stated: "Soviet citizen Bozer ... communicated to the Deputy naval attaché that, according to a statement of a certain German officer from Hitler's headquarters, Germany is preparing to invade the USSR on May 14 through Finland, the Baltic countries and Latvia. At the same time Moscow and Leningrad will be heavily raided and paratroopers landed in border cities...."

In his report of May 22, 1941, the Deputy Military Attaché in Berlin, Khlopov, communicated that "...the attack of the German Army is reportedly scheduled for June 15, but it is possible that it may begin in the first days of June..."

A cable from our London Embassy dated June 18, 1941 stated: "As of now Cripps is deeply convinced of the inevitability of armed conflict between Germany and the USSR, which will begin not later than the middle of June. According to Cripps, the Germans have presently concentrated 147 divisions (including air force and service units) along the Soviet borders...."

Despite these particularly grave warnings, the necessary steps were not taken to prepare the country properly for defense and to prevent it from being caught unawares.

Did we have time and the capabilities for such preparations? Yes, we had the time and the capability. Our industry was already so developed that it was capable of supplying fully the Soviet Army with everything that it needed. This is proven by the fact that, although during the war we lost almost half of our industry and important industrial and food-production areas as the result of enemy occupation of the Ukraine, Northern Caucasus and other western parts of the country, the Soviet nation was still able to organize the production of military equipment in the eastern parts of the country, to install there equipment taken from the western industrial areas, and to supply our armed forces with everything necessary to destroy the enemy.

Had our industry been mobilized properly and in time to supply the Army with the necessary materiel, our wartime losses would have been decidedly smaller. However such mobilization had not been started in time. And already in the first days of the war it became evident that our Army was badly armed. We did not have enough artillery, tanks and planes to throw the enemy back.

Soviet science and technology produced excellent models of

tanks and artillery pieces before the war. But mass production of all this was not organized. As a matter of fact, we started to modernize our military equipment only on the eve of the war. As a result, when the enemy invaded Soviet territory we did not have sufficient quantities either of old machinery which was no longer used for armament production or of new machinery which we had planned to introduce into armament production.

The situation with anti-aircraft artillery was especially bad. We did not organize the production of anti-tank ammunition. Many fortified regions proved to be indefensible as soon as they were attacked, because their old arms had been withdrawn and new ones were not yet available there.

This pertained, alas, not only to tanks, artillery and planes. At the outbreak of the war we did not even have sufficient numbers of rifles to arm the mobilized manpower. I recall that in those days I telephoned from Kiev to comrade [Georgy] Malenkov and told him, "People have volunteered for the new Army [units] and are demanding weapons. You must send us arms."

Malenkov answered me, "We cannot send you arms. We are sending all our rifles to Leningrad and you have to arm yourselves."

(Movement in the hall.)

Such was the armament situation.

In this connection we cannot forget, for instance, the following fact: Shortly before the invasion of the Soviet Union by Hitler's army, [Colonel-General M. P.] Kirponos, who was chief of the Kiev Special Military District (he was later killed at the front), wrote to Stalin that German armies were at the Bug River, were preparing for an attack and in the very near future would probably start their offensive. In this connection, Kirponos proposed that a strong defense be organized, that 300,000 people be evacuated from the border areas and that several strong points be organized there: anti-tank ditches, trenches for the soldiers, etc.

Moscow answered this proposition with the assertions that this would be a provocation, that no preparatory defensive work should be undertaken at the borders, and that the Germans were not to be given any pretext for the initiation of military action against us. Thus our borders were insufficiently prepared to repel the enemy.

When the fascist armies had actually invaded Soviet territory and military operations began, Moscow issued an order that German fire was not to be returned. Why? It was because Stalin, despite the self-evident facts, thought that the war had not yet started, that this was only a provocative action on the part of several undisciplined sections of the German Army, and that our reaction might serve as a reason for the Germans to begin the war.

The following fact is also known: On the eve of the invasion of Soviet territory by Hitler's army, a certain German citizen crossed our border and stated that the German armies had received orders to start [their] offensive against the Soviet Union on the night of June 22 at 3 o'clock. Stalin was informed about this immediately, but even this warning was ignored.

As you see, everything was ignored: warnings of certain Army commanders, declarations of deserters from the enemy army, and even the open hostility of the enemy. Is this an example of the alertness of the chief of the Party and of the state at this particularly significant historical moment?

And what were the results of this carefree attitude, this disregard of clear facts? The result was that already in the first hours and days the enemy had destroyed in our border regions a large part of our Air Force, our artillery and other military equipment. [Stalin] annihilated large numbers of our military cadres and disorganized our military leadership. Consequently we could not prevent the enemy from marching deep into the country.

Very grievous consequences, especially with regard to the beginning of the war, followed Stalin's annihilation of many military commanders and political workers during 1937-1941 because of his suspiciousness and through slanderous accusations. During these years repressions were instituted against certain parts of our military cadres beginning literally at the company- and battalion-commander levels and extending to higher military centers. During this time, the cadre of leaders who had gained military experience in Spain and in the Far East was almost completely liquidated.

The policy of large-scale repression against military cadres led also to undermined military discipline, because for several years officers of all ranks and even soldiers in Party and Komsomol cells were taught to "unmask" their superiors as hidden enemies.

(Movement in the hall.)

It is natural that this caused a negative influence on the state of military discipline in the initial stage of the war.

And, as you know, we had before the war excellent military cadres which were unquestionably loyal to the Party and to the Fatherland. Suffice it to say that those of them who managed to survive, despite severe tortures to which they were subjected in the prisons, have from the first war days shown themselves real patriots and heroically fought for the glory of the Fatherland. I have here in mind such [generals] as: [Konstantin] Rokossovsky (who, as you know, had been jailed); [Alexander] Gorbatov; [Kiril] Meretskov (who is a delegate at the present Congress); [K. P.] Podlas (he was an excellent commander who perished at the front); and many, many others. However, many such commanders perished in the camps and the jails and the Army saw them no more.

All this brought about a situation at the beginning of the war that was a great threat to our Fatherland.

It would be wrong to forget that, after [our] severe initial disaster[s] and defeat[s] at the front, Stalin thought that it was the end. In one of his [declarations] in those days he said: "Lenin left us a great legacy and we've lost it forever."

After this Stalin for a long time actually did not direct military operations and ceased to do anything whatsoever. He returned to active leadership only when a Politburo delegation visited him and told him that steps needed to be taken immediately so as to improve the situation at the front.

Therefore, the threatening danger which hung over our Fatherland in the initial period of the war was largely due to Stalin's very own faulty methods of directing the nation and the Party.

However, we speak not only about the moment when the war began, which led to our Army's serious disorganization and brought us severe losses. Even after the war began, the nervousness and hysteria which Stalin demonstrated while interfering with actual military operations caused our Army serious damage.

Stalin was very far from understanding the real situation that was developing at the front. This was natural because, during the whole Patriotic War, he never visited any section of the front or any liberated city except for one short ride on the Mozhaisk highway during a stabilized situation at the front. To this incident were dedicated many literary works full of fantasies of all sorts and so many paintings. Simultaneously, Stalin was interfering with operations and issuing orders which did not take into consideration the real situation at a given section of the front and which could not help but result in huge personnel losses.

I will allow myself in this connection to bring out one characteristic fact which illustrates how Stalin directed operations at the fronts. Present at this Congress is Marshal [Ivan] Bagramyan, who was once the head of operations in the

Southwestern Front Headquarters and who can corroborate what I will tell you.

When an exceptionally serious situation for our Army developed in the Kharkov region in 1942, we correctly decided to drop an operation whose objective was to encircle [the city]. The real situation at that time would have threatened our Army with fatal consequences if this operation were continued.

We communicated this to Stalin, stating that the situation demanded changes in [our] operational plans so that the enemy would be prevented from liquidating a sizable concentration of our Army.

Contrary to common sense, Stalin rejected our suggestion. He issued the order to continue the encirclement of Kharkov, despite the fact that at this time many [of our own] Army concentrations actually were threatened with encirclement and liquidation.

I telephoned to [Marshal Alexander] Vasilevsky and begged him: "Alexander Mikhailovich, take a map" – Vasilevsky is present here – "and show comrade Stalin the situation that has developed." We should note that Stalin planned operations on a globe.

(Animation in the hall.)

Yes, comrades, he used to take a globe and trace the front line on it. I said to comrade Vasilevsky: "Show him the situation on a map. In the present situation we cannot continue the operation which was planned. The old decision must be changed for the good of the cause."

Vasilevsky replied, saying that Stalin had already studied this problem. He said that he, Vasilevsky, would not see Stalin further concerning this matter, because the latter didn't want to hear any arguments on the subject of this operation.

After my talk with Vasilevsky, I telephoned to Stalin at his *dacha*. But Stalin did not answer the phone and Malenkov was at the receiver. I told comrade Malenkov that I was calling from the front and that I wanted to speak personally to Stalin. Stalin informed me through Malenkov that I should speak with Malenkov. I stated for the second time that I wished to inform Stalin personally about the grave situation which had arisen for us at the front. But Stalin did not consider it convenient to pick up the phone and again stated that I should speak to him through Malenkov, although he was only a few steps from the telephone.

After "listening" in this manner to our plea, Stalin said: "Let everything remain as it is!"

And what was the result of this? The worst we had expected. The Germans surrounded our Army concentrations and as a result [the Kharkov counterattack] lost hundreds of thousands of our soldiers. This is Stalin's military "genius." This is what it cost us.

(Movement in the hall.)

On one occasion after the war, during a meeting [between] Stalin [and] members of the Politburo, Anastas Ivanovich Mikoyan mentioned that Khrushchev must have been right when he telephoned concerning the Kharkov operation and that it was unfortunate that his suggestion had not been accepted.

You should have seen Stalin's fury! How could it be admitted that he, Stalin, had not been right! He is after all a "genius," and a genius cannot help but be right! Everyone can err, but Stalin considered that he never erred, that he was always right. He never acknowledged to anyone that he made any mistake, large or small, despite the fact that he made more than a few in matters of theory and in his practical activity. After the Party Congress we shall probably have to re-evaluate many [of our] wartime military operations and present them in their true light.

The tactics on which Stalin insisted – without knowing the basics of conducting battle operations – cost much blood until we succeeded in stopping the opponent and going over to the offensive.

The military knows that as late as the end of 1941, instead of great operational maneuvers flanking [our] opponent and penetrating behind his back, Stalin was demanding incessant frontal [counter-]attacks and the [re-]capture of one village after another.

Because of this, we paid with great losses – until our generals, upon whose shoulders the whole weight of conducting the war rested, succeeded in altering the situation and shifting to flexible-maneuver operations. [This] immediately brought serious changes at the front [that were] favorable to us.

All the more shameful was the fact that after our great victory over the enemy, which cost us so dearly, Stalin began to downgrade many of the commanders who had contributed so much to it. [This was] because Stalin ruled out any chance that services rendered at the front might be credited to anyone but himself.

Stalin was very much interested in assessments of comrade [Grigory] Zhukov as a military leader. He asked me often for my opinion of Zhukov. I told him then, "I have known Zhukov for a long time. He is a good general and a good military leader."

After the war Stalin began to tell all kinds of nonsense about Zhukov. Among it [was] the following: "You praised Zhukov, but he does not deserve it. They say that before each operation at the front Zhukov used to behave as follows: He used to take a handful of earth, smell it and say, 'We can begin the attack,' or its opposite, 'The planned operation cannot be carried out.'" I stated at the time, "Comrade Stalin, I do not know who invented this, but it is not true."

It is possible that Stalin himself invented these things for the purpose of minimizing the role and military talents of Marshal Zhukov.

In this connection, Stalin very energetically popularized himself as a great leader. In various ways he tried to inculcate the notion that the victories gained by the Soviet nation during the

Great Patriotic War were all due to the courage, daring, and genius of Stalin and of no one else. Just like [a] Kuzma Kryuchkov, he put one dress on seven people at the same time.

(Animation in the hall.)

In the same vein, let us take for instance our historical and military films and some [of our] literary creations. They make us feel sick. Their true objective is propagating the theme of praising Stalin as a military genius. Let us recall the film, *The Fall of Berlin*. Here only Stalin acts. He issues orders in a hall in which there are many empty Chairs. Only only one man approaches him to report something to him – it is [Alexander] Poskrebyshev, his loyal shield-bearer.

(Laughter in the hall.)

And where is the military command? Where is the Politburo? Where is the Government? What are they doing, and with what are they engaged? There is nothing about them in the film. Stalin acts for everybody, he does not reckon with anyone. He asks no one for advice. Everything is shown to the people in this false light. Why? To surround Stalin with glory– contrary to the facts and contrary to historical truth.

The question arises: Where is the military, on whose shoulders rested the burden of the war? It is not in the film. With Stalin's inclusion, there was no room left for it.

Not Stalin, but the Party as a whole, the Soviet Government, our heroic Army, its talented leaders and brave soldiers, the whole

Soviet nation – these are the ones who assured victory in the Great Patriotic War.

(Tempestuous and prolonged applause.)

Central Committee members, Ministers, our economic leaders, the leaders of Soviet culture, directors of territorial-party and Soviet organizations, engineers, and technicians – every one of them in his own place of work generously gave of his strength and knowledge toward ensuring victory over the enemy.

Exceptional heroism was shown by our hard core – surrounded by glory are our whole working class, our kolkhoz peasantry, the Soviet intelligentsia, who under the leadership of Party organizations overcame untold hardships and bearing the hardships of war, and devoted all their strength to the cause of the Fatherland's defense.

Our Soviet women accomplished great and brave deeds during the war. They bore on their backs the heavy load of production work in the factories, on the kolkhozes, and in various economic and cultural sectors. Many women participated directly in the Great Patriotic War at the front. Our brave youth contributed immeasurably, both at the front and at home, to the defense of the Soviet Fatherland and to the annihilation of the enemy.

The services of Soviet soldiers, of our commanders and political workers of all ranks are immortal. After the loss of a considerable part of the Army in the initial war months, they did not lose their heads and were able to reorganize during the course of combat. Over the course of the war they created and toughened a strong, heroic Army. They not only withstood [our] strong and cunning enemy's pressure but smashed him.

The magnificent, heroic deeds of hundreds of millions of people of the East and of the West during the fight against the threat of fascist subjugation which loomed before us will live for centuries, [indeed] for millennia in the memory of thankful humanity.

(Thunderous applause.)

The main roles and the main credit for the victorious ending of the war belong to our Communist Party, to the armed forces of the Soviet Union, and to the tens of millions of Soviet people uplifted by the Party.

(Thunderous and prolonged applause.)

Comrades, let us reach for some other facts. The Soviet Union justly is considered a model multinational state because we have assured in practice the equality and friendship of all [of the] peoples living in our great Fatherland.

All the more monstrous are those acts whose initiator was Stalin and which were rude violations of the basic Leninist principles [behind our] Soviet state's nationalities policies. We refer to the mass deportations of entire nations from their places of origin, together with all Communists and Komsomols without any exception. This deportation was not dictated by any military considerations.

Thus, at the end of 1943, when there already had been a permanent change of fortune at the front in favor of the Soviet Union, a decision concerning the deportation of all the Karachai from the lands on which they lived was taken and executed.

In the same period, at the end of December, 1943, the same lot befell the [Kalmyks] of the Kalmyk Autonomous Republic. In March, 1944, all the Chechens and Ingushi were deported and the Chechen-Ingush Autonomous Republic was liquidated. In April, 1944, all Balkars were deported from the territory of the Kabardino-Balkar Autonomous Republic to faraway places and their Republic itself was renamed the Autonomous Kabardian Republic.

Ukrainians avoided meeting this fate only because there were too many of them and there was no place to which to deport them. Otherwise, [Stalin] would have deported them also.

(Laughter and animation in the hall.)

No Marxist-Leninist, no man of common sense can grasp how it is possible to make whole nations responsible for inimical activity, including women, children, old people, Communists and Komsomols, to use mass repression against them, and to expose them to misery and suffering for the hostile acts of individual persons or groups of persons.

After the conclusion of the Patriotic War, the Soviet nation proudly stressed the magnificent victories gained through [our] great sacrifices and tremendous efforts. The country experienced a period of political enthusiasm. The Party came out of the war even more united. Its cadres were tempered and hardened by the fire of the war. Under such conditions nobody could have even thought of the possibility of some plot in the Party.

And it was precisely at this time that the so-called "Leningrad affair" was born. As we have now proven, this case was fabricated. Those who innocently lost their lives included: comrades [Nikolay] Voznesensky, [Aleksey] Kuznetsov, [Mikhail] Rodionov, [Pyotr] Popkov, and others.

As is known, Voznesensky and Kuznetsov were talented and eminent leaders. Once they stood very close to Stalin. It is sufficient to mention that Stalin made Voznesensky First Deputy to the Chairman of the Council of Ministers and Kuznetsov was elected Secretary of the Central Committee. The very fact that Stalin entrusted Kuznetsov with the supervision of the state-security organs shows the trust which he enjoyed.

How did it happen that these persons were branded as enemies of the people and liquidated?

Facts prove that the "Leningrad affair" is also the result of willfulness which Stalin exercised against Party cadres. Had a normal situation existed in the Party's Central Committee and in the Central Committee Politburo, affairs of this nature would have been examined there in accordance with Party practice, and all pertinent facts assessed; as a result, such an affair as well as others would not have happened.

We must state that, after the war, the situation became even more complicated. Stalin became even more capricious, irritable and brutal. In particular, his suspicion grew. His persecution mania reached unbelievable dimensions. Many workers became enemies before his very eyes. After the war, Stalin separated himself from the collective even more. Everything was decided by him alone without any consideration for anyone or anything.

This unbelievable suspicion was cleverly taken advantage of by the abject provocateur and vile enemy, Beria, who murdered thousands of Communists and loyal Soviet people. The elevation of Voznesensky and Kuznetsov alarmed Beria. As we have now proven, it had been precisely Beria who had "suggested" to Stalin the fabrication by him and by his confidants of materials in the form of declarations and anonymous letters, and in the form of various rumors and talks.

The Party's Central Committee has examined this so-called "Leningrad affair"; persons who innocently suffered are now rehabilitated and honor has been restored to the glorious Leningrad Party organization. [V. S.] Abakumov and others who had fabricated this affair were brought before a court; their trial took place in Leningrad and they received what they deserved.

The question arises: Why is it that we see the truth of this affair only now, and why did we not do something earlier, during Stalin's life, in order to prevent the loss of innocent lives? It was because Stalin personally supervised the "Leningrad affair," and the majority of the Politburo members did not, at that time, know all of the circumstances in these matters and could not therefore intervene.

When Stalin received certain material from Beria and Abakumov, without examining these slanderous materials he ordered an investigation of the "affair" of Voznesensky and Kuznetsov. With this, their fate was sealed.

Similarly instructive is the case of the Mingrelian nationalist organization which supposedly existed in Georgia. As is known, resolutions by the Central Committee, Communist Party of the Soviet Union, were made concerning this case in November 1951 and in March 1952. These resolutions were made without prior discussion with the Politburo. Stalin had personally dictated them. They made serious accusations against many loyal Communists. On the basis of falsified documents, it was proven that there existed in Georgia a supposedly nationalistic organization whose objective was the liquidation of the Soviet power in that republic with the help of imperialist powers.

In this connection, a number of responsible Party and Soviet workers were arrested in Georgia. As was later proven, this was a slander directed against the Georgian Party organization.

We know that there have been at times manifestations of local bourgeois nationalism in Georgia as in several other republics. The question arises: Could it be possible that, in the period during which the resolutions referred to above were made, nationalist tendencies grew so much that there was a danger of Georgia's leaving the Soviet Union and joining Turkey?

(Animation in the hall, laughter).

This is, of course, nonsense. It is impossible to imagine how such assumptions could enter anyone's mind. Everyone knows how Georgia has developed economically and culturally under Soviet rule. Industrial production in the Georgian Republic is 27 times greater than it was before the Revolution. Many new industries have arisen in Georgia which did not exist there before the Revolution: iron smelting, an oil industry, a machine-construction industry, etc. Illiteracy has long since been liquidated, which, in pre-Revolutionary Georgia, included 78 per cent of the population.

Could the Georgians, comparing the situation in their republic with the hard situation of the working masses in Turkey, be aspiring to join Turkey? In 1955, Georgia produced 18 times as much steel per person as Turkey. Georgia produces 9 times as much electrical energy per person as Turkey. According to the available 1950 census, 65 per cent of Turkey's total population is illiterate, and 80 per cent of its women. Georgia has 19 institutions of higher learning which have about 39,000 students; this is 8 times more than in Turkey (for each 1,000 inhabitants). The prosperity of the working people has grown tremendously in Georgia under Soviet rule.

It is clear that, as the economy and culture develop, and as the socialist consciousness of the working masses in Georgia grows, the source from which bourgeois nationalism draws its strength evaporates.

As it developed, there was no nationalistic organization in Georgia. Thousands of innocent people fell victim to willfulness and lawlessness. All of this happened under the "genius" leadership of Stalin, "the great son of the Georgian nation," as Georgians like to refer to him.

(Animation in the hall.)

The willfulness of Stalin showed itself not only in decisions concerning the internal life of the country but also in the international relations of the Soviet Union.

The July Plenum of the Central Committee studied in detail the reasons for the development of conflict with Yugoslavia. It was a shameful role which Stalin played here. The "Yugoslav affair" contained no problems which could not have been solved through Party discussions among comrades. There was no significant basis for the development of this "affair." It was completely possible to have prevented the rupture of relations with that country. This does not mean, however, that Yugoslav leaders made no mistakes or had no shortcomings. But these mistakes and shortcomings were magnified in a monstrous manner by Stalin, resulting in the breakoff of relations with a friendly country.

I recall the first days when the conflict between the Soviet Union and Yugoslavia began to be blown up artificially. Once, when

I came from Kiev to Moscow, I was invited to visit Stalin, who, pointing to the copy of a letter recently sent to [Yugoslavian President Marshal Joseph] Tito, asked me, "Have you read this?"

Not waiting for my reply, he answered, "I will shake my little finger – and there will be no more Tito. He will fall."

We have paid dearly for this "shaking of the little finger." This statement reflected Stalin's mania for greatness, but he acted just that way: "I will shake my little finger – and there will be no Kosior"; "I will shake my little finger once more and Postyshev and Chubar will be no more"; "I will shake my little finger again – and Voznesensky, Kuznetsov and many others will disappear."

But this did not happen to Tito. No matter how much or how little Stalin shook, not only his little finger but everything else that he could shake, Tito did not fall. Why? The reason was that, in this instance of disagreement with [our] Yugoslav comrades, Tito had behind him a state and a people who had had a serious education in fighting for liberty and independence, a people who gave support to its leaders.

You see what Stalin's mania for greatness led to. He completely lost consciousness of reality. He demonstrated his suspicion and haughtiness not only in relation to individuals in the USSR, but in relation to whole parties and nations.

We have carefully examined the case of Yugoslavia. We have found a proper solution which is approved by the peoples of the Soviet Union and of Yugoslavia as well as by the working masses of all the people's democracies and by all progressive humanity. The liquidation of [our] abnormal relationship with Yugoslavia was done in the interest of the whole camp of socialism, in the interest of strengthening peace in the whole world.

Let us also recall the "affair of the doctor-plotters."

(Animation in the hall.)

Actually there was no "affair" outside of the declaration of the woman doctor [Lidiya] Timashuk, who was probably influenced or ordered by someone (after all, she was an unofficial collaborator of the organs of state security) to write Stalin a letter in which she declared that doctors were applying supposedly improper methods of medical treatment.

Such a letter was sufficient for Stalin to reach an immediate conclusion that there are doctor-plotters in the Soviet Union. He issued orders to arrest a group of eminent Soviet medical specialists. He personally issued advice on the conduct of the investigation and the method of interrogation of the arrested persons. He said that academician [V. N.] Vinogradov should be put in chains, and that another one [of the alleged plotters] should be beaten. The former Minister of State Security, comrade [Semyen] Ignatiev, is present at this Congress as a delegate. Stalin told him curtly, "If you do not obtain confessions from the doctors we will shorten you by a head."

(Tumult in the hall.)

Stalin personally called the investigative judge, gave him instructions, and advised him on which investigative methods should be used. These methods were simple – beat, beat and, beat again.

Shortly after the doctors were arrested, we members of the Politburo received protocols with the doctors' confessions of guilt. After distributing these protocols, Stalin told us, "You are blind like young kittens. What will happen without me? The country will perish because you do not know how to recognize enemies."

The case was presented so that no one could verify the facts on which the investigation was based. There was no possibility of trying to verify facts by contacting those who had made the confessions of guilt.

We felt, however, that the case of the arrested doctors was questionable. We knew some of these people personally because they had once treated us. When we examined this "case" after Stalin's death, we found it to have been fabricated from beginning to end.

This ignominious "case" was set up by Stalin. He did not, however, have the time in which to bring it to an end (as he conceived that end), and for this reason the doctors are still alive. All of them have been rehabilitated. They are working in the same places they were working before. They are treating top individuals, not excluding members of the Government. They have our full confidence; and they execute their duties honestly, as they did before.

In putting together various dirty and shameful cases, a very base role was played by a rabid enemy of our Party, an agent of a foreign intelligence service – Beria, who had stolen into Stalin's confidence. How could this provocateur have gained such a position in the Party and in the state, so as to become the First Deputy Chair of the Council of Ministers of the Soviet Union and a Politburo member? It has now been established that this villain climbed up the Government ladder over an untold number of corpses.

Were there any signs that Beria was an enemy of the Party? Yes, there were. Already in 1937, at a Central Committee Plenum, former People's Commissar of Health [Grigory] Kaminsky said that Beria worked for the Musavat intelligence service. But the Plenum had barely concluded when Kaminsky was arrested and then shot. Had Stalin examined Kaminsky's statement? No, because Stalin believed in Beria, and that was enough for him. And when Stalin believed in anyone or anything, then no one could say anything that was contrary to his opinion. Anyone daring to express opposition would have met the same fate as Kaminsky.

There were other signs, also. The declaration which comrade [A. V.] Snegov made to the Party's Central Committee isinteresting. (Parenthetically speaking, he was also rehabilitated not long ago, after 17 years in prison camps.) In this declaration, Snegov writes:

"In connection with the proposed rehabilitation of the former Central Committee member, [Lavrenty] Kartvelishvili-Lavrentiev, I have entrusted to the hands of the representative of the Committee of State Security a detailed deposition concerning Beria's role in the disposition of the Kartvelishvili case and concerning the criminal motives by which Beria was guided.

"In my opinion, it is indispensable to recall an important fact pertaining to this case and to communicate it to the Central Committee, because I did not consider it as proper to include in the investigation documents.

"On October 30, 1931, at a session of the Organizational Bureau of the Central Committee of the All-Union Communist Party (Bolsheviks), Kartvelishvili, Secretary of the Transcaucasian Regional Committee, made a report. All members of the executive of the Regional Committee were present. Of them I alone am now alive.

"During this session, J. V. Stalin made a motion at the end of his speech concerning the organization of the secretariat of the Transcaucasian Regional Committee composed of the following: First Secretary, Kartvelishvili; Second Secretary, Beria (it was then, for the first time in the Party's history, that Beria's name was mentioned as a candidate for a Party position). Kartvelishvili answered that he knew Beria well and for that reason refused categorically to work together with him. Stalin proposed then that this matter be left open and that it be solved in the process of the work itself. Two days later a decision was arrived at that Beria would receive the Party post and that Kartvelishvili would be deported from the Transcaucasus.

"This fact can be confirmed by comrades Mikoyan and Kaganovich, who were present at that session."

The long, unfriendly relations between Kartvelishvili and Beria were widely known. They date back to the time when comrade Sergo [Ordzhonikidze] was active in the Transcaucasus. Kartvelishvili was the closest assistant of Sergo. The unfriendly relationship impelled Beria to fabricate a "case" against Kartvelishvili. It is characteristic that Kartvelishvili was charged with a terroristic act against Beria in this "case."

The indictment in the Beria case contains a discussion of his crimes. Some things should, however, be recalled, especially since it is possible that not all delegates to the Congress have read this document. I wish to recall Beria's bestial disposition of the cases of [Mikhail] Kedrov, [V.] Golubev, and Golubev's adopted mother, Baturina – persons who wished to inform the Central Committee concerning Beria's treacherous activity. They were shot without any trial and the sentence was passed ex post facto, after the execution.

Here is what the old Communist, comrade Kedrov, wrote to the Central Committee through comrade [Andrey] Andreyev (comrade Andreyev was then a Central Committee Secretary):

"I am calling to you for help from a gloomy cell of the Lefortovo prison. Let my cry of horror reach your ears; do not remain deaf, take me under your protection; please, help remove the nightmare of interrogations and show that this is all a mistake.

"I suffer innocently. Please believe me. Time will testify to the truth. I am not an agent provocateur of the Tsarist Okhrana. I am not a spy, I am not a member of an anti-Soviet organization of which I am being accused on the basis of denunciations. I am also not guilty of any other crimes against the Party and the Government. I am an old Bolshevik, free of any stain; I have honestly fought for almost 40 years in the ranks of the Party for the good and prosperity of the nation....

"... Today I, a 62-year-old man, am being threatened by the investigative judges with more severe, cruel and degrading methods of physical pressure. They (the judges) are no longer capable of becoming aware of their error and of recognizing that their handling of my case is illegal and impermissible. They try to justify their actions by picturing me as a hardened and raving enemy and are demanding increased repressions. But let the Party know that I am innocent and that there is nothing which can turn a loyal son of the Party into an enemy, even right up to his last dying breath.

"But I have no way out. I cannot divert from myself the hastily approaching new and powerful blows.

"Everything, however, has its limits. My torture has reached the extreme. My health is broken, my strength and my energy are waning, the end is drawing near. To die in a Soviet prison, branded as a vile traitor to the Fatherland – what can be more monstrous for an honest man? And how monstrous all this is! Unsurpassed bitterness and pain grips my heart. No! No! This will not happen; this cannot be, I cry. Neither the Party, nor the Soviet Government, nor the People's Commissar, L. P. Beria, will permit this cruel, irreparable injustice. I am firmly certain that, given a quiet, objective examination, without any foul rantings, without any anger and without the fearful tortures, it would be easy to prove the baselessness of the charges. I believe deeply that truth and justice will triumph. I believe. I believe."

The old Bolshevik, comrade Kedrov, was found innocent by the Military Collegium. But, despite this, he was shot at Beria's order.

(Indignation in the hall.)

Beria also handled cruelly the family of comrade Ordzhonikidze. Why? Because Ordzhonikidze had tried to prevent

Beria from realizing his shameful plans. Beria had cleared from his way all persons who could possibly interfere with him. Ordzhonikidze was always an opponent of Beria, which he told to Stalin. Instead of examining this affair and taking appropriate steps, Stalin allowed the liquidation of Ordzhonikidze's brother and brought Ordzhonikidze himself to such a state that he was forced to shoot himself.

(Indignation in the hall.)

Beria was unmasked by the Party's Central Committee shortly after Stalin's death. As a result of particularly detailed legal proceedings, it was established that Beria had committed monstrous crimes and Beria was shot.

The question arises why Beria, who had liquidated tens of thousands of Party and Soviet workers, was not unmasked during Stalin's life. He was not unmasked earlier because he had utilized very skillfully Stalin's weaknesses; feeding him with suspicions, he assisted Stalin in everything and acted with his support.

Comrades: The cult of the individual acquired such monstrous size chiefly because Stalin himself, using all conceivable methods, supported the glorification of his own person. This is supported by numerous facts. One of the most characteristic examples of Stalin's self-glorification and of his lack of even elementary modesty is the edition of his *Short Biography*, which was published in 1948 (sic).

This book is an expression of the most dissolute flattery, an example of making a man into a godhead, of transforming him into an infallible sage, "the greatest leader, sublime strategist of all times and nations." Finally, no other words could be found with which to lift Stalin up to the heavens.

We need not give here examples of the loathesome adulation filling this book. All we need to add is that they all were approved and edited by Stalin personally. Some of them were added in his own handwriting to the draft text of the book.

What did Stalin consider essential to write into this book? Did he want to cool the ardor of the flatterers who were composing his *Short Biography*? No! He marked the very places where he thought that the praise of his services was insufficient. Here are some examples characterizing Stalin's activity, added in Stalin's own hand:

> "In this fight against the skeptics and capitulators, the Trotskyites, Zinovievites, Bukharinites and Kamenevites, there was definitely welded together, after Lenin's death, that leading core of the Party... that upheld the great banner of Lenin, rallied the Party behind Lenin's behests, and brought the Soviet people onto the broad paths of industrializing the country and collectivizing the rural economy. The leader of this core and the guiding force of the Party and the state was comrade Stalin."

Thus writes Stalin himself! Then he adds:

> "Although he performed his tasks as leader of the Party and the people with consummate skill, and enjoyed the unreserved support of the entire Soviet people, Stalin never allowed his work to be marred by the slightest hint of vanity, conceit or self-adulation."

Where and when could a leader so praise himself? Is this worthy of a leader of the Marxist-Leninist type? No. Precisely against this did Marx and Engels take such a strong position. This always was sharply condemned also by Vladimir Ilyich Lenin.

In the draft text of [Stalin's] book appeared the following sentence: "Stalin is the Lenin of today." This sentence appeared to Stalin to be too weak. Thus, in his own handwriting, he changed it to read: "Stalin is the worthy continuer of Lenin's work, or, as it is said in our Party, Stalin is the Lenin of today." You see how well it is said, not by the nation but by Stalin himself.

It is possible to offer many such self-praising appraisals written into the draft text of that book in Stalin's hand. He showers himself especially generously with praises regarding his military genius and his talent for strategy. I will cite one more insertion made by Stalin on the theme: "The advanced Soviet science of war received further development," he writes, "at Comrade Stalin's hands. Comrade Stalin elaborated the theory of the permanent operating factors that decide the issue of wars, of active defense and the laws of counteroffensive and offensive, of the cooperation of all services and arms in modern warfare, of the role of big tank masses and air forces in modern war, and of the artillery as the most formidable of the armed services. At various stages of the war, Stalin's genius found correct solutions that took into account all the circumstances of the situation."

(Movement in the hall.)

Further, Stalin writes: "Stalin's military mastership was displayed both in defense and on offense. Comrade Stalin's genius enabled him to divine the enemy's plans and defeat them. The battles in which comrade Stalin directed the Soviet armies are brilliant examples of operational military skill."

This is how Stalin was praised as a strategist. Who did this? Stalin himself, not in his role as a strategist but in the role of an author-editor, one of the main creators of his [own] self-adulatory biography. Such, comrades, are the facts. Or should be said, rather, the shameful facts.

One additional fact from the same *Short Biography* of Stalin: As is known, the *History of the All-Union Communist Party (Bolsheviks), Short Course* was written by a commission of the Party Central Committee.

This book, parenthetically, was also permeated with the cult of the individual and was written by a designated group of authors. This fact was reflected in the following formulation on the proof copy of the *Short Biography* of Stalin: "A commission of the Central Committee, All-Union Communist Party (Bolsheviks), under the direction of comrade Stalin and with his most active personal participation, has prepared a *History of the All-Union Communist Party (Bolsheviks), Short Course.*"

But even this phrase did not satisfy Stalin: The following sentence replaced it in the final version of the *Short Biography*: "In 1938, the book *History of the All-Union Communist Party (Bolsheviks), Short Course* appeared, written by comrade Stalin and approved by a commission of the Central Committee, All-Union Communist Party (Bolsheviks)." Can one add anything more?

(Animation in the hall.)

As you see, a surprising metamorphosis changed the work created by a group into a book written by Stalin. It is not necessary to state how and why this metamorphosis took place.

A pertinent question comes to our mind: If Stalin is the author of this book, why did he need to praise the person of Stalin so much and to transform the whole post-October historical period of our glorious Communist Party solely into an action of "the Stalin genius"?

Did this book properly reflect the efforts of the Party in the socialist transformation of the country, in the construction of socialist society, in the industrialization and collectivization of the country, and also other steps taken by the Party which undeviatingly traveled the path outlined by Lenin? This book speaks principally about Stalin, about his speeches, about his reports. Everything without the smallest exception is tied to his name.

And when Stalin himself asserts that he himself wrote the *Short Course,* this calls at least for amazement. Can a Marxist-Leninist thus write about himself, praising his own person to the heavens?

Or let us take the matter of the Stalin Prizes.

(Movement in the hall.)

Not even the Tsars created prizes which they named after themselves.

Stalin recognized as the best a text of the national anthem of the Soviet Union which contains not a word about the Communist Party; it contains, however, the following unprecedented praise of Stalin: "Stalin brought us up in loyalty to the people. He inspired us to great toil and deeds."

In these lines of the anthem, the whole educational, directional and inspirational activity of the great Leninist Party is ascribed to Stalin. This is, of course, a clear deviation from Marxism-Leninism, a clear debasing and belittling of the role of the Party. We should add for your information that the Presidium of the Central Committee has already passed a resolution concerning the composition of a new text of the anthem. which will reflect the role of the people and the role of the Party.

(Loud, prolonged applause.)

And was it without Stalin's knowledge that many of the largest enterprises and towns were named after him? Was it without his knowledge that Stalin monuments were erected in the whole country – these "memorials to the living"? It is a fact that Stalin himself had signed on July 2, 1951 a resolution of the USSR Council of Ministers concerning the erection on the Volga-Don Canal of an impressive monument to Stalin; on September 4 of the same year he issued an order making 33 tons of copper available for the construction of this impressive monument.

Anyone who has visited the Stalingrad area must have seen the huge statue which is being built there, and that on a site which hardly any people frequent. Huge sums were spent to build it at a time when people of this area had lived since the war in huts. Consider, yourself, was Stalin right when he wrote in his biography that "...he did not allow in himself... even a shadow of conceit, pride, or self-adoration"?

At the same time Stalin gave proofs of his lack of respect for Lenin's memory. It is not a coincidence that, despite the decision taken over 30 years ago to build a Palace of Soviets as a monument to Vladimir Ilyich, this palace was not built, its construction was always postponed and the project allowed to lapse.

We cannot forget to recall the Soviet Government resolution of August 14, 1925 concerning "the founding of Lenin prizes for educational work." This resolution was published in the press, but until this day there are no Lenin prizes. This, too, should be corrected.

(Tumultuous, prolonged applause.)

During Stalin's life – thanks to known methods which I have mentioned, and quoting facts, for instance. from the *Short Biography* of Stalin – all events were explained as if Lenin played only a secondary role, even during the October Socialist Revolution. In many films and in many literary works the figure of Lenin was incorrectly presented and inadmissibly depreciated.

Stalin loved to see the film *The Unforgettable Year of 1919*, in which he was shown on the steps of an armored train and where he was practically vanquishing the foe with his own saber. Let Klimenty Yefremovich [Voroshilov], our dear friend, find the necessary courage and write the truth about Stalin; after all, he knows how Stalin had fought. It will be difficult for comrade Voroshilov to undertake this, but it would be good if he did it. Everyone will approve of it, both the people and the Party. Even his grandsons will thank him.

(Prolonged applause.)

In speaking about the events of the October Revolution and about the Civil War, the impression was created that Stalin always played the main role, as if everywhere and always Stalin had suggested to Lenin what to do and how to do it. However, this is slander of Lenin.

(Prolonged applause.)

I will probably not sin against the truth when I say that 99 per cent of the persons present here heard and knew very little about Stalin before the year 1924, while Lenin was known to all. He was known to the whole Party, to the whole nation, from children all the way up to old men.

(Tumultuous, prolonged applause.)

All this has to be thoroughly revised so that history, literature and the fine arts properly reflect V. I. Lenin's role and the great deeds of our Communist Party and of the Soviet people – a creative people.

(Applause.)

Comrades! The cult of the individual caused the employment of faulty principles in Party work and in economic activity. It brought about rude violation of internal Party and Soviet democracy, sterile administration, deviations of all sorts, cover-ups of shortcomings, and varnishings of reality. Our nation bore forth many flatterers and specialists in false optimism and deceit.

We should also not forget that, due to the numerous arrests of Party, Soviet and economic leaders, many workers began to work uncertainly, showed overcautiousness, feared all which was new, feared their own shadows, and began to show less initiative in their work.

Take, for instance, Party and Soviet resolutions. They were

prepared in a routine manner, often without considering the concrete situation. This went so far that Party workers, even during the smallest sessions, read [prepared] speeches. All this produced the danger of formalizing the Party and Soviet work and of bureaucratizing the whole apparatus.

Stalin's reluctance to consider life's realities, and the fact that he was not aware of the real state of affairs in the provinces, can be illustrated by his direction of agriculture.

All those who interested themselves even a little in the national situation saw the difficult situation in agriculture, but Stalin never even noted it. Did we tell Stalin about this? Yes, we told him, but he did not support us. Why? Because Stalin never traveled anywhere, did not meet city and kolkhoz workers. He did not know the actual situation in the provinces.

He knew the country and agriculture only from films. And these films dressed up and beautified the existing situation in agriculture. Many films pictured kolkhoz life such that [farmhouse] tables groaned from the weight of turkeys and geese. Evidently, Stalin thought that it was actually so.

Vladimir Ilyich Lenin looked at life differently. He always was close to the people. He used to receive peasant delegates and often spoke at factory gatherings. He used to visit villages and talk with the peasants.

Stalin separated himself from the people and never went anywhere. This lasted ten years. The last time he visited a village was in January, 1928, when he visited Siberia in connection with grain procurements. How then could he have known the situation in the provinces?

Once, [Stalin] was told during a discussion that our situation on the land was a difficult one and that the situation in cattle breeding and meat production was especially bad. [From this] there came a commission charged with the preparation of a resolution called "Measures toward the further development of animal husbandry in kolkhozes and sovkhozes." We worked out this project.

Of course, our proposals at that time did not cover all the possibilities. However we did chart ways in which animal husbandry on kolkhozes and sovkhozes could be boosted. We proposed to raise livestock prices so as to create material incentives for kolkhoz, MTS [machine-tractor station] and sovkhoz workers in developing breeding. But our project was not accepted, In February 1953 it was laid aside entirely.

What is more, while reviewing this project Stalin proposed that the taxes paid by kolkhozes and by kolkhoz workers should be raised by 40 billion rubles. According to him, the peasants were well off and a kolkhoz worker would need to sell only one more chicken to pay his tax in full.

Think about what this implied. Forty billion rubles is a sum which [these workers] did not realize for *all* the products which they sold to the State. In 1952, for instance, kolkhozes and kolkhoz workers received 26,280 million rubles for all products delivered and sold to the State.

Did Stalin's position, then, rest on data of any sort whatever? Of course not. In such cases facts and figures did not interest him. If Stalin said anything, it meant it was so – after all, he was a "genius," and a genius does not need to count, he only needs to look and can immediately tell how it should be. When he expresses his opinion, everyone has to repeat it and to admire his wisdom.

But how much wisdom was contained in the proposal to raise the agricultural tax by 40 billion rubles? None, absolutely none, because the proposal was not based on an actual assessment of the situation but on the fantastic ideas of a person divorced from reality.

We are currently beginning slowly to work our way out of a difficult agricultural situation. The speeches of the delegates to the Twentieth Congress please us all. We are glad that many delegates have delivered speeches [to the effect] that conditions exist for fulfilling the sixth Five-Year Plan for animal husbandry [early]: not in five years, but within two to three years. We are certain that the commitments of the new Five-Year Plan will be accomplished successfully.

(Prolonged applause.)

Comrades! If we sharply criticize today the cult of the individual which was so widespread during Stalin's life, and if we

102

speak about the many negative phenomena generated by this cult (which is so alien to the spirit of Marxism-Leninism), some may ask: How could it be? Stalin headed the Party and the country for 30 years and many victories were gained during his lifetime. Can we deny this? In my opinion, the question can be asked in this manner only by those who are blinded and hopelessly hypnotized by the cult of the individual, only by those who do not understand the essence of the revolution and of the Soviet state, only by those who do not understand, in a Leninist manner, the role of the Party and of the nation in the development of the Soviet society.

[Our] Socialist Revolution was attained by the working class and by the poor peasantry with the partial support of middle-class peasants. It was attained by the people under the leadership of the Bolshevik Party. Lenin's great service consisted of the fact that he created a militant Party of the working class, but he was armed with Marxist understanding of the laws of social development and with the science of proletarian victory in the fight with capitalism, and he steeled this Party in the crucible of the revolutionary struggle of the masses of the people.

During this fight the Party consistently defended the interests of the people and became its experienced leader. [The Party] led the working masses to power, to the creation of the first socialist state. You remember well the wise words of Lenin: that the Soviet state is strong because of the awareness of the masses that history is created by the millions and tens of millions of people.

Our historical victories were attained thanks to the Party's organizational work, to the many provincial organizations, and to the self-sacrificing work of our great nation. These victories are the result of the great drive and activity of the nation and of the Party as a whole. They are not at all the fruit of Stalin's leadership, which is how the situation was pictured during the period of the cult of the individual.

If we are to consider this matter as Marxists and as Leninists, then we have to state unequivocally that the leadership practices which came into being during the last years of Stalin's life became a serious obstacle in the path of Soviet social development. Stalin often failed for months to take up some unusually important problems, concerning the life of the Party and of the State, whose solution could not be postponed. During Stalin's leadership our peaceful relations with other nations were often threatened, because one-man decisions could cause, and often did cause, great complications.

In the past [few] years, [after] we managed to free ourselves of the harmful practice of the cult of the individual and took several proper steps in terms of [both] internal and external policies, everyone [has been able to see] how activity has grown before our very eyes, how the creative activity of the broad working masses has developed, and how favorably all this has acted upon economic and cultural development.

(Applause.)

Some comrades may ask us: Where were the members of the Politburo? Why did they not assert themselves against the cult of the individual in time? And why is this being done only now? First of all, we have to consider the fact that the members of the Politburo viewed these matters in a different way at different times. Initially, many of them backed Stalin actively because he was one of the strongest Marxists and his logic, his strength and his will greatly influenced [Party] cadres and Party work.

It is known that after Lenin's death, especially during the first years, Stalin actively fought for Leninism against the enemies of Leninist theory and against those who deviated. Beginning with Leninist theory, the Party, with its Central Committee at the head, started on a great scale work on the socialist industrialization of the country, on agricultural collectivization, and on cultural revolution. At that time Stalin gained great popularity, sympathy and support. The Party had to fight those who tried to lead the country away from the correct Leninist path. It had to fight Trotskyites, Zinovievites and rightists, and bourgeois nationalists. This fight was indispensable.

Later, however, Stalin, abusing his power more and more, began to fight eminent Party and Government leaders and to use terroristic methods against honest Soviet people. As we have already shown, Stalin thus handled such eminent Party and State leaders as Kosior, Rudzutak, Eikhe, Postyshev and many others.

Attempts to oppose groundless suspicions and charges

resulted in the opponent's falling victim to the repression. This characterized the fall of comrade Postyshev.

In one of his [exchanges] Stalin expressed his dissatisfaction with Postyshev and asked him, "What are you actually?"

Postyshev answered clearly, "I am a Bolshevik, comrade Stalin, a Bolshevik."

At first, this assertion was considered to show [merely] a lack of respect for Stalin. Later it was considered a harmful act. Eventually it resulted in Postyshev's annihilation and castigation as an "enemy of the people."

In the situation which then prevailed, I often talked with Nikolay Alexandrovich Bulganin. Once when we two were traveling in a car, he said, "It has happened sometimes that a man goes to Stalin on his invitation as a friend. And when he sits with Stalin, he does not know where he will be sent next – home or to jail."

It is clear that such conditions put every member of the Politburo in a very difficult situation. And, when we also consider the fact that in the last years Central Committee Plenary sessions were not convened and that sessions of the Politburo occurred only occasionally, from time to time, then we will understand how difficult it was for any member of the Politburo to take a stand against one or another unjust or improper procedure, against serious errors and shortcomings in leadership practices.

As we have already shown, many decisions were taken

either by one person or in a roundabout way, without collective discussion. The sad fate of Politburo member comrade Voznesensky, who fell victim to Stalin's repressions, is known to all. Characteristically, the decision to remove him from the Politburo was never discussed but was reached in a devious fashion. In the same way came the decision regarding Kuznetsov's and Rodionov's removals from their posts.

The importance of the Central Committee's Politburo was reduced and its work was disorganized by the creation within the Politburo of various commissions – the so-called "quintets," "sextets," "septets" and "nonets" Here is, for instance, a Politburo resolution from October 3, 1946:

"Stalin's proposal:

"1.The Politburo Commission for Foreign Affairs ('Sextet') is to concern itself in the future, in addition to foreign affairs, also with matters of internal construction and domestic policy.

"2.The Sextet is to add to its roster the Chairman of the State Commission of Economic Planning of the USSR, comrade Voznesensky, and is to be known as a Septet.

"Signed: Secretary of the Central Committee, J. Stalin."

What [sophistry]!

(Laughter in the hall.)

It is clear that the creation within the Politburo of this type of commissions – "quintets," "sextets," "septets" and "nonets" – was against the principle of collective leadership. The result of this was that some members of the Politburo were in this way kept away from participation in reaching the most important state matters.

One of the oldest members of our Party, Klimenty Yefremovich Voroshilov, found himself in an almost impossible situation. For several years he was actually deprived of the right of participation in Politburo sessions. Stalin forbade him to attend Politburo sessions and to receive documents. When the Politburo was in session and comrade Voroshilov heard about it, he telephoned each time and asked whether he would be allowed to attend. Sometimes Stalin permitted it, but always showed his dissatisfaction.

Because of his extreme suspicion, Stalin toyed also with the absurd and ridiculous suspicion that Voroshilov was an English agent.

(Laughter in the hall.)

It's true – an English agent. A special tap was installed in his home to listen to what was said there.

(Indignation in the hall.)

By unilateral decision, Stalin had also separated one other man from the work of the Politburo – Andrey Andreyevich Andreyev. This was one of the most unbridled acts of willfulness.

Let us consider the first Central Committee Plenum after the 19th Party Congress. Stalin, in his talk at the Plenum, characterized Vyacheslav Mikhailovich Molotov and Anastas Ivanovich Mikoyan and suggested that these old workers of our Party were guilty of some baseless charges. We cannot rule out the possibility that had Stalin remained at the helm for another several months, Comrades Molotov and Mikoyan probably would not have delivered any speeches at this [20th] Congress.

Stalin evidently had plans to finish off the older members of the Politburo. He often stated that Politburo members should be replaced by new ones. His proposal after the 19th Congress to elect 25 persons to the Central Committee Presidium was aimed at the removal of old Politburo members and at bringing in less experienced persons so that these would extol him in all sorts of ways.

We can assume that this was also a design for the future annihilation of the old Politburo members and, in this way, a cover for all shameful acts of Stalin, acts which we are now considering.

Comrades! So as not to repeat errors of the past, the Central Committee has declared itself resolutely against the cult of the individual. We consider that Stalin was extolled to excess. However, in the past Stalin undoubtedly performed great services to the

Party, to the working class and to the international workers' movement.

This question is complicated by the fact that all this which we have just discussed was done during Stalin's life under his leadership and with his concurrence; here Stalin was convinced that this was necessary for the defense of the interests of the working classes against the plotting of enemies and against the attack of the imperialist camp.

He saw this from the position of the interest of the working class, of the interest of the laboring people, of the interest of the victory of socialism and communism. We cannot say that these were the deeds of a giddy despot. He considered that this should be done in the interest of the Party, of the working masses, in the name of the defense of the revolution's gains. In this lies the whole tragedy!

Comrades! Lenin had often stressed that modesty is an absolutely integral part of a real Bolshevik. Lenin himself was the living personification of the greatest modesty. We cannot say that we have been following this Leninist example in all respects.

It is enough to point out that many towns, factories and industrial enterprises, kolkhozes and sovkhozes, Soviet institutions and cultural institutions have been referred to by us with a title if I may express it so – of private property of the names of these or those Government or Party leaders who were still active and in good health. Many of us participated in the action of assigning our names to various towns, rayons, enterprises and kolkhozes. We must correct this.

(Applause.)

But this should be done calmly and slowly. The Central Committee will discuss this matter and consider it carefully in order to prevent errors and excesses. I can remember how Ukraine learned about Kossior's arrest. Kiev radio used to start its programs thus: "This is Radio Kosior." When one day the programs began without mentioning Kosior, everyone was quite certain that something had happened to him and that he probably had been arrested.

Thus, if today we begin to change the signs everywhere and to rename things, people will think that these comrades in whose honor the given enterprises, kolkhozes or cities are named also met some bad fate and that they have also been arrested.

(Animation in the hall.)

How is the authority and the importance of this or that leader judged? On the basis of how many towns, industrial enterprises and factories, kolkhozes and sovkhozes carry his name. Is it not about time that we eliminate this "private property" and "nationalize" the factories, the industrial enterprises, the kolkhozes and the sovkhozes? (Laughter, applause, voices: "That is right.") This will benefit our cause. After all, the cult of the individual is manifested also in this way.

We should, in all seriousness, consider the question of the

111

cult of the individual. We cannot let this matter get out of the Party, especially not to the press. It is for this reason that we are considering it here at a closed Congress session. We should know the limits; we should not give ammunition to the enemy; we should not wash our dirty linen before their eyes. I think that the delegates to the Congress will understand and assess properly all these proposals.

(Tumultuous applause.)

Comrades! We must abolish the cult of the individual decisively, once and for all; we must draw the proper conclusions concerning both ideological-theoretical and practical work. It is necessary for this purpose:

First, in a Bolshevik manner to condemn and to eradicate the cult of the individual as alien to Marxism-Leninism and not consonant with the principles of Party leadership and the norms of Party life, and to fight inexorably all attempts at bringing back this practice in one form or another.

To return to and actually practice in all our ideological work the most important theses of Marxist-Leninist science about the people as the creator of history and as the creator of all material and spiritual good of humanity, about the decisive role of the Marxist Party in the revolutionary fight for the transformation of society, about the victory of communism.

In this connection we will be forced to do much work in order to examine critically from the Marxist-Leninist viewpoint and to correct the widely spread erroneous views connected with the cult of the individual in the spheres of history, philosophy, economy and of other sciences, as well as in literature and the fine arts. It is especially necessary that in the immediate future we compile a serious textbook of the history of our Party which will be edited in accordance with scientific Marxist objectivism, a textbook of the history of Soviet society, a book pertaining to the events of the Civil War and the Great Patriotic War.

Second, to continue systematically and consistently the work done by the Party's Central Committee during the last years, a work characterized by minute observation in all Party organizations, from the bottom to the top, of the Leninist principles of Party leadership, characterized, above all, by the main principle of collective leadership, characterized by the observance of the norms of Party life described in the statutes of our Party, and, finally, characterized by the wide practice of criticism and self-criticism.

Third, to restore completely the Leninist principles of Soviet socialist democracy, expressed in the Constitution of the Soviet Union, to fight willfulness of individuals abusing their power. The evil caused by acts violating revolutionary socialist legality which have accumulated during a long time as a result of the negative influence of the cult of the individual has to be completely corrected.

Comrades! The 20th Congress of the Communist Party of

the Soviet Union has manifested with a new strength the unshakable unity of our Party, its cohesiveness around the Central Committee, its resolute will to accomplish the great task of building communism.

(Tumultuous applause.)

And the fact that we present in all their ramifications the basic problems of overcoming the cult of the individual which is alien to Marxism-Leninism, as well as the problem of liquidating its burdensome consequences, is evidence of the great moral and political strength of our Party.

(Prolonged applause.)

We are absolutely certain that our Party, armed with the historical resolutions of the 20th Congress, will lead the Soviet people along the Leninist path to new successes, to new victories.

(Tumultuous, prolonged applause.)

Long live the victorious banner of our Party – Leninism!

(Tumultuous, prolonged applause ending in ovation. All rise.)

End U.S. Aggression Against the Republic of Cuba

The following letter was written to US President John F Kennedy

Mr. President, I send you this message in an hour of alarm, fraught with danger for the peace of the whole world. Armed aggression has begun against Cuba. It is a secret to no one that the armed bands invading this country were trained, equipped and armed in the United States of America. The planes which are bombing Cuban cities belong to the United States of America, the bombs they are dropping are being supplied by the American Government.

All of this evokes here in the Soviet Union an understandable feeling of indignation on the part of the Soviet Government and the Soviet people.

Only recently, in exchanging opinions through our respective representatives, we talked with you about the mutual desire of both sides to put forward joint efforts directed toward improving relations between our countries and eliminating the danger of war.

Your statement a few days ago that the USA would not participate in military activities against Cuba created the impression that the top leaders of the United States were taking into account the consequences for general peace and for the USA itself which aggression against Cuba could have. How can what is being done by the United States in reality be understood, when an attack on Cuba has now become a fact?

It is still not late to avoid the irreparable. The Government of the USA still has the possibility of not allowing the flame of war ignited by interventions in Cuba to grow into an incomparable conflagration. I approach you, Mr. President, with an urgent call to put an end to aggression against the Republic of Cuba. Military armament and the world political situation are such at this time that any so-called "little war" can touch off a chain reaction in all parts of the globe.

As far as the Soviet Union is concerned, there should be no mistake about our position: We will render the Cuban people and their government all necessary help to repel armed attack on Cuba. We are sincerely interested in a relaxation of international tension, but if others proceed toward sharpening, we will answer them in full measure. And in general it is hardly possible so to conduct matters that the situation is settled in one area and conflagration extinguished, while a new conflagration is ignited in another area.

I hope that the Government of the USA will consider our

views as dictated by the sole concern not to allow steps which could lead the world to military catastrophe.

Moscow, April 18, 1961

Of What Freedom Are you Speaking?

The following letter was written to US President John F Kennedy

Mr. President,

I have received your reply of April 18. You write that the United States intends no military intervention in Cuba. But numerous facts known to the whole world — and to the Government of the United States, of course, better than to any one else — speak differently. Despite all assurances to the contrary, it has now been proved beyond doubt that it was precisely the United States which prepared the intervention, financed its arming and transported the gangs of mercenaries that invaded the territory of Cuba.

United States armed forces also took a direct part in the accomplishment of the gangster attack upon Cuba. American bombers and fighters supported the operations of the mercenaries who landed on Cuban territory, and participated in the military operations against the armed forces of the lawful Government and people of Cuba.

Such are the facts. They bear witness to direct United States participation in the armed aggression against Cuba.

In your message you took the course of justifying, and even lauding, the attack on Cuba — this crime which has revolted the entire world. You try to justify the organization of a military attack on Cuba, committed for the sole reason that the way of life chosen by its people is not to the taste of the ruling circles of the United States and the North American monopolies operating in Latin America, by talk about the United States Government's adherence to the ideals of "freedom". But, one may ask, of what freedom are you speaking?

Of freedom to strangle the Cuban people with the bony hand of hunger through the establishment of an economic blockade? Is that freedom?

Of freedom to send military planes over the territory of Cuba, to subject peaceful Cuban cities to barbarous bombing, to set fire to sugar-cane plantations? Is that freedom?

History records many cases in which, on the pretext of defending freedom, peoples have been drowned in blood, colonial wars waged, and one small nation after another taken by the throat.

In the present case, apparently, the United States Government is seeking to restore to Cuba that "freedom" under which Cuba would dance to the tune of her more powerful neighbour and foreign monopolies would again be able to plunder the country's national wealth, to wax rich on the sweat and blood of the Cuban people. But it is precisely against such "freedom" that the Cuban people accomplished their revolution when they threw out Batista, who may have loyally served the interests of his foreign masters but who was a foreign element in the body of the Cuban nation.

You, Mr. President, display concern for a handful of enemies who were expelled by their people and found refuge under the wing of those who want to keep the guns of their cruisers and destroyers trained on Cuba. But why are you not concerned about the fate of the six million Cuban people, why do you not wish to pay regard to their inalienable right to a free and independent life, their right to arrange their domestic affairs as they see fit? Where are the standards of international law, or even of simple human morality, that would justify such a position? They simply do not exist.

The Cuban people have once again expressed their will with a clarity which should have left no room for doubt, even in the minds of those who prefer to close their eyes to reality. They have shown that they not only know their interests, but can stand up for them. Cuba today is not, of course, the Cuba you identify with the handful of traitors who have come out against their people. It is the Cuba of workers, peasants and intellectuals, it is a people which has rallied round its revolutionary Government headed by the national hero, Fidel Castro. And, judging from everything, this people received the interventionists in a fitting way. Is not this convincing proof of the real will of the Cuban people?

I think it is. And since this is so, is it not time for all to draw from it the right conclusions?

As for the Soviet Union, we have stated on many occasions, and I now state again, that our Government does not seek any advantages or privileges in Cuba. We have no bases in Cuba, and we do not intend to establish any. And this is well known to you, to your generals and your admirals. If, despite this, they still try to frighten the people by fabrications about "Soviet bases" on Cuba, that is obviously designed for consumption by simpletons. But there are fewer and fewer such simpletons, and that applies also, I hope, to the United States.

By the way, Mr. President, I would like to express my opinion concerning the statements made by you and by certain other United States politicians to the effect that rockets and other weapons could be installed on Cuban territory for possible use against the United States.

The inference from this is that the United States has some alleged right to attack Cuba, either directly or through the traitors to the Cuban people whom you arm with your weapons, train on your territory, maintain with the money of United States taxpayers and transport with the resources of your armed forces, covering them from the air and the sea while they fight against the Cuban people and their lawful government.

You also refer to some United States obligations to protect

the Western hemisphere against external aggression. But what obligations can possibly apply in the present case? No one can have any obligations to defend rebels against the lawful government of a sovereign State, such as Cuba is.

Mr. President, you are setting out on a very dangerous road. Think of it. You speak of your rights and obligations, and, of course, anyone can claim this or that right. But then you will have to admit that other States, too, can base their actions in similar circumstances on similar arguments and considerations.

You allege that Cuba cannot lend her territory for actions against the United States. That is your supposition, but it is based on no facts. We, on the other hand, can already refer to concrete facts, not suppositions: in some countries, bordering on the Soviet Union by land and sea, there are at present Governments following a policy that is far from reasonable, Governments which have concluded military agreements with the United States and have made their territory available for the establishment of American military bases. And your military say openly that these bases are spearheaded against the Soviet Union, as if this were not already sufficiently clear. So, if you consider yourself entitled to take such measures against Cuba as the United States Government has been resorting to lately, you must admit that other countries have no lesser grounds for acting in the same way with regard to States whose territories are the scene of actual preparations constituting a threat to the security of the Soviet Union. If you do not want to sin against elementary logic, you must obviously concede this right to other States. We, for our part, do not hold such views. We consider that the arguments advanced on this score in the United States constitute, not merely an extremely free interpretation of international law, but, to put it plainly, open advocacy of a treacherous policy.

A powerful State can of course always find a pretext for attacking a weaker country, and then justify its attack by claiming that that country was a potential menace. But is this twentieth-century morality? This is the morality of the colonialists, of the brigands who once pursued precisely such a policy. Today, in the second half of the twentieth century, it is no longer possible to take the pirate morality of the colonialists as a guide. We all see, today, how the colonial system is crumbling and becoming a thing of the past. The Soviet Union, for its part, is doing everything to promote this process, and we are proud of it.

Or take the United States actions with regard to China. What standards of law can be invoked to justify these actions? Everyone knows that Taiwan is an inalienable part of China. This has been admitted even by the Government of the United States, whose signature appears on the Cairo Declaration of 1943. But later the United States seized Taiwan — took, in fact, the road to brigandage. The People's Republic of China announced its natural aspiration to reunite the territory of Taiwan with the rest of Chinese territory. But how did the United States react to this? It declared that it would use armed force to prevent reunification of this Chinese territory, seized by it, with the rest of China. It threatens war if China takes any steps towards the recovery of Taiwan. And this is being done by a country which has officially recognized that Taiwan belongs to China! Is not this perfidy in international relations? If such methods were to become the rule in relations between States, there would be no place left for law. Its place would be taken by lawlessness and arbitrariness.

So, Mr. President, your sympathies are one thing; but actions against the security and independence of other peoples, taken on the basis of such sympathies, are very much another. You may, of course, express your sympathy with the imperialist and colonialist countries; that does not surprise anyone. For example, you vote with them in the United Nations. This is a matter of your morality. But what has been done against Cuba is no longer morality. It is gangsterism.

I should like to stress that if the United Nations is really to become strong and fulfil the functions for which it was established — and at present this Organization, unfortunately, is a body already infected by the bacilli of colonialism and imperialism — the United Nations must resolutely condemn the banditry undertaken against Cuba. And the point here is not merely to condemn the United States. The important thing is that the condemnation of aggression should be seen to be a precedent, a lesson which other countries, too, might learn, so that aggression should never again be repeated. For if we were to take the course of approving or even, simply, condoning the morality of the aggressors, it could be adopted by other States as well, and this would inevitably lead to military conflicts, any of which might result in a third world war.

What you said in your last statement to the Press must fill the entire world with great alarm. For you simply claim, in fact, some right of yours to employ military force whenever you find it necessary, and to suppress other peoples each time you decide that their expression of their will constitutes "communism". But what right have you, what right has anyone in general, to deprive a people of the possibility of choosing their social and political system of their own free will? Have you never considered that other countries, too, might perhaps advance a demand similar to yours and might declare that you, in the United States, have a system which breeds wars and espouses an imperialist policy, the policy of threats and attacks against other countries? There is every ground for such accusations. And, proceeding from the principles which you now proclaim, one could, apparently, demand a change in the internal system of the United States. We, as you know, do not follow that road. We favour the peaceful coexistence of all States, and non-interference in the internal affairs of other countries.

You allude to Budapest. But we can tell you openly, without any allusions: it is you, the United States, that crushed the independence of Guatemala by sending your mercenaries there, as you are now trying to do with regard to Cuba. It is the United States, and no other country, that still mercilessly exploits and keeps in economic bondage the countries of Latin America and many other countries of the world. This is known to all. And if, Mr. President, your logic is to be followed, actions from without could apparently be organized against your country too, to put an end forever to this imperialist policy, the policy of threats, the policy of suppressing the freedom-loving peoples.

As for your concern for the emigres expelled by the Cuban people, I should like to add the following. You are of course well aware that there are, in many countries, emigres who are dissatisfied with the situation and the system existing in the countries from which they fled. And if the abnormal practice were introduced, in relations between States, of using these emigres, especially with arms in their hand, against the countries they had fled from, it can be openly said that this would inevitably lead to conflicts and wars. It would therefore be well to refrain from such ill-advised actions. This is a slippery and dangerous road which can lead to a new world war.

In your reply, you saw fit to touch upon certain questions unrelated to the subject of my message to you, including the question — as interpreted by you — of the historic inevitability of a communist revolution. I can only regard this as an attempt to evade the main question — that of aggression against Cuba. We are prepared, in appropriate circumstances, to exchange opinions on the question of the ways in which human society develops, although this question cannot be settled by debates between groups or individuals, however high their position may be. The question of whose system is the better will be decided by history, by the peoples themselves.

You, Mr. President, speak often and much of your desire that Cuba should be free. But that attitude is flatly contradicted by all United States actions with regard to this small country, let alone the latest armed attack upon Cuba organized with a view to changing Cuba's internal system by force. It was the United States which nearly 60 years ago imposed on Cuba the enslaving terms of the Havana Treaty and established its Guantanamo naval base on Cuban territory. Yet the United States is the most powerful country in the Western hemisphere, and no one in that hemisphere can threaten you with a military invasion. Consequently, if you continue to retain your naval base on Cuban territory against the clearly expressed will of the Cuban people and its Government, it is because this base is designed, not to serve as a defense against an attack by any external forces, but to suppress the will of the Latin American peoples. It was established to fulfil the functions of a gendarme, to keep the peoples of Latin America politically and economically dependent.

The Government of the United States is now fulminating against Cuba. But this indicates only one thing — your lack of trust in your own system, in the policy pursued by the United States. And this is understandable, as it is a policy of exploitation, a policy for the economic enslavement of under-developed countries. You have no confidence in your own system, and therefore fear that Cuba's example may prove contagious for other countries. But aggressive, bandit actions cannot save your system. In the historic process of the development of human society, each people decides, and will

127

decide, its own destiny.

As for the Soviet Union, the peoples of our country settled this question finally and irrevocably over 43 years ago. We constitute a socialist state. Our social system is the most equitable of all that have so far existed, because in our country all the means of production are owned by those who work. That is indeed a contagious example, and the sooner the need to go over to this system is realized, the sooner will the whole of mankind achieve a really just society. By this very development, an end will be put, once and for all, to war.

You, Mr. President, did not like it when I said, in my previous message, that there can be no stable place in the world if anywhere war is aflame. But this is really so. The world is a single whole, whether we like it or not. And I can only repeat what I said: it is impossible to proceed by adjusting the situation and putting out the flames in one area, and kindling a new conflagration in another.

The Soviet State has always been a consistent defender of the freedom and independence of all peoples. We naturally, therefore, cannot concede to the United States any right to control the destinies of other countries, including the countries of Latin America. We consider that any interference by one State in the affairs of another — especially armed interference — is a violation of all international laws and of the principles of peaceful coexistence which the Soviet Union has invariably upheld since the first days of its existence.

If it is now, more than ever before, the duty of every State and its leaders not to permit actions which are capable of jeopardizing universal peace, that applies with all the more force to the leaders of the great Powers. It is this that I urge upon you, Mr. President.

The Soviet Government's position in international affairs remains unchanged. We wish to build our relations with the United States in such a way that neither the Soviet Union nor the United States, as the two most powerful countries in the world, shall engage in sabre-rattling or push their military or economic superiority to the forefront, since that would lead to an aggravation of the international situation, not to its improvement. We are sincerely desirous of reaching agreement, both with you and with other countries of the world, on disarmament and all the other questions whose solution would promote peaceful coexistence, the recognition of every people's right to the social and political systems established by it, genuine respect for the will of the peoples and non-interference in their internal affairs. Only under these conditions can one really speak of coexistence, for coexistence is possible only if States with different social systems obey international laws and recognize the maintenance of world peace as their highest aim. Only in that event will peace be based on firm foundations.

Moscow, April 22, 1961

On the Cessation of Nuclear Testing, U.S. Occupation of West Berlin, U.S. Aggression against Cuba

The following letter was written to US President John F Kennedy

I studied with interest your reply [Documents 55 and 53] to my considerations forwarded through Ambassador Dobrynin on the question of cessation of nuclear weapon tests.

It is said in your reply that a serious effort should be made to work out by January 1, 1963 an agreement on the question of cessation of nuclear weapon tests. Well, I can say quite definitely that we will not make you wait. The Soviet Union in the course of many years has been pressing for concluding an agreement on cessation of all nuclear weapon tests and we are prepared to make new efforts in this direction for the sake of achieving this aim.

The Soviet Government is convinced that national means of detecting nuclear explosions now at the disposal of the states are quite adequate to ensure strict control over the fulfillment by all states of their commitments with regard to cessation of nuclear weapon tests in the atmosphere, in outer space and under water as well as underground. And the U.S. too recognizes this now with respect to three types of tests — in the atmosphere, in outer space and under water — and no longer insists on establishing international control over the cessation of these tests. Thus there seems to be no difference between us on this point any longer. There remains the question of underground tests. In the U.S. doubts are still being expressed as to the adequacy of national means for detecting underground tests. We do not have such doubts. Nevertheless we are prepared to use every opportunity to come to an agreement on this question on a mutually acceptable basis, on such a basis that would remove your doubts.

I do not know whether you have noticed a suggestion of British scientists Bullard and Penney put forward at the recent Pugwash conference of scientists [Reference is to Sir Edward Bullard and Sir William Penney and the 10th Pugwash Conference on Science and World Affairs held in London September 3-7.] concerning the use of automatic seismic stations working without any personnel. As we understood, the idea of this suggestion is that automatic seismic stations help with their records to determine what is the cause of this or that underground tremor — underground nuclear blasts or ordinary earthquakes. It would be a sort of mechanical control without men. After thinking this suggestion over we came to the conclusion that it can be accepted if this would make it easier to reach an agreement. In this case it could be provided in the treaty banning all nuclear weapon tests that automatic seismic stations be set up both near the borders of the nuclear states and 2-3 such stations directly on the territory of the states possessing nuclear weapons — in the areas most frequently subjected to earthquakes.

The Soviet Government agrees to this only because it seeks a mutually acceptable basis for an agreement. We do not intend to violate the commitment that we assume regarding cessation of tests but we also want to make you and the public opinion of the U.S. to feel confident that all sides will display an honest approach in fulfilling this commitment.

If you agree to this then we could without much difficulty come to an agreement on cessation of all nuclear weapon tests.

I would like to view as an encouraging sign the fact that the American scientists who took part in the Pugwash conference — and as I was told, very prominent ones — approved of the suggestion about the use of automatic seismic stations for the purposes of control. The Soviet scientists — participants in the Pugwash conference — also approved of this suggestion. So it appears that the scientists are already in agreement. Then there is a possibility to move ahead quickly. And as for us, we would like very much to put an end to all that and reach, at last, an agreement on cessation of nuclear tests of all kinds. There have been enough — both for us and for you — of experimental blasts carried out in the atmosphere and underground.

If we can come now to the conclusion of an agreement on cessation of all nuclear weapon tests we will make good for the peoples of our countries and for the peoples of the entire world.

We prefer to conclude now a treaty on cessation of all nuclear weapon tests. But if the Western powers are not yet prepared for that even taking into account the suggestions put forward at the Pugwash conference we, as I have already told you, are ready in this case also to make a step toward the Western powers and to conclude at this time a treaty on cessation of nuclear weapon tests in three environments: in the atmosphere, in outer space and under water.

It would be incorrect in doing that to leave open the question of underground nuclear tests. For it would create a false impression with the world public opinion, a kind of illusion, that an agreement on cessation of tests has seemingly been concluded and that the competition among states in perfecting nuclear arms in coming to an end whereas in fact this competition would continue. The weapons already created would be remodeled on the basis of new scientific data obtained as a result of experimental underground blasts, that is the states would replenish their arsenals with ever more perfect, ever more destructive types of nuclear weapons. With that we cannot agree. I must say frankly and openly that it is impossible to agree to conclude an agreement on the basis of tests in the atmosphere, in outer space and under water if the United States intends to continue underground nuclear explosions. Since in this case we too would face a necessity to carry out experimental nuclear weapon tests and we would conduct those tests, as we are doing now, in the atmosphere.

What is the way out? From our previous exchange of opinion you know how we propose to overcome this difficulty — to agree that after a treaty banning nuclear tests in the atmosphere, in outer space and under water is signed, negotiations on cessation of underground tests as well should be continued and while these suggestions are in progress and until the agreement is reached all nuclear powers should refrain from conducting such tests.

But some people in the West do not want even to hear about any commitment by the states to refrain from conducting nuclear tests. And on the part of some statesmen and in the American press assertions are made from time to time that the Soviet Union has allegedly violated some agreement on moratorium on nuclear tests. However those who make such statements have neither proof nor ground to support them.

And what are the facts? No international agreement on moratorium on underground or any other nuclear tests ever existed and nobody ever signed such an agreement. It can be reminded that as early as March 31, 1958 the Soviet Union unilaterally discontinued tests of all kinds of atomic and hydrogen weapons and called upon the Western powers to follow its example. But the U.S. and Britain responded then to that proposal of ours with an unprecedented in scope new series of tests of nuclear bombs. In subsequent period since the end of 1958 neither the United States or Britain nor the Soviet Union conducted nuclear weapon tests, but they acted so not because of any obligations coming from an international agreement but because of their own unilateral decisions. However, as early as December 29, 1959 your predecessor President Eisenhower clearly and definitely stated that the U.S. did not consider itself any longer bound by its statement that it had no intention to conduct nuclear tests. As for France — a NATO ally of the U.S. and Britain — it was even at that time conducting one nuclear explosion after another.

All this is perfectly known and he who nevertheless claims that the Soviet Union allegedly violated some moratorium on nuclear tests either has a short memory or simply seeks to torpedo the conclusion of an agreement on cessation of nuclear weapon tests.

I would like to note with satisfaction that now you seem to agree in principle that along with the conclusion of a treaty on the ban of nuclear weapon tests in the atmosphere, in outer space and under water a moratorium with regard to underground explosions be accepted. If this is so, then it opens certain prospects.

You believe at the same time, as I have understood, that there should be no unlimited moratorium on underground tests. But we do not put the question that way. We do not propose to declare an unlimited moratorium on underground explosions. We suggest to declare such moratorium for a certain period of time, while the negotiations on banning underground tests of nuclear weapons are in progress. For how long those negotiations will go on — it is of course, impossible to say. But we do not think that much time is needed to conclude a final agreement on underground tests, provided, of course, that both sides display interest in reaching such an agreement promptly.

Anyway we are ready to agree on a term for the course of which the states will assume commitments not to conduct underground nuclear explosions, if an agreement banning nuclear tests only in the atmosphere, in outer space and under water is reached. We agree, for instance, on a 5-year term. And during the five years it will certainly be possible to agree on a final solution of the question of banning also underground nuclear explosions though, I repeat, I am convinced that it could be done much faster, especially if the idea of use for the purposes of control of automatic seismic stations is acceptable to you. During this period of time, one should assume, all American scientists too will get convinced that the national means of detection of nuclear explosions are quite adequate for assuring a foolproof control over cessation of nuclear tests, underground tests included.

If, however, even during that term an agreement is not reached — what to do in this case? Then the whole question of banning nuclear weapon tests will have to be reconsidered anew. And if the American side then insists on renewing underground nuclear tests, then — I want to say this already now and in plain terms — the Soviet Union will consider itself free from assumed obligations not to conduct nuclear tests in the atmosphere, in outer space and under water.

These are considerations which came to my mind in

connection with your reply on the question of cessation of nuclear weapon tests. Giving you these considerations I think of nothing else but how to move from the dead point, and out of deadlock, the question of cessation of nuclear weapon tests.

If you being concerned about the same are in agreement with our considerations let me know and then the Soviet representatives in Geneva will at once be given instructions to get down together with your and British representatives to practical work of preparing a draft agreement.

One cannot doubt that an agreement on cessation of nuclear weapon tests would be greeted with tremendous joy by all mankind. The peoples wherever they live — in Europe or America, in Africa, Asia or Australia — desire peace, a lasting peace, they want an end to the nuclear arms race, they want the threat of nuclear war be eliminated.

U.S. Occupation of West Berlin

During his meeting with Ambassador Dobrynin Robert Kennedy referring to you, Mr. President, confidentially touched upon the problem of Soviet-American relations. He said in particular that you are concerned with the worsening of these relations. We ourselves are very much upset about that but we would like to draw your attention to the fact that the aggravation of relations between the Soviet Union and the United States was not sown by us and it was not we who started it. We have sincerely sought and continue to seek to do everything for the normalization of our relations and not only for normalization but for their radical betterment. But that is being hindered by the hot-beds of international tension which are a source of constant friction between our countries. They should be removed and, first of all, the abnormal situation in West Berlin should be done away with.

I believe that you, Mr. President, like me realize that until a reasonable solution is reached on West Berlin this source will always make our relations feverish. And under present circumstances we do not see any other way out but to sign a German peace treaty. On this basis it would be possible with no loss to the prestige of either side to solve the problem of West Berlin too, to guarantee, as you say, the freedom of the population of West Berlin by stationing there for some not very long time a certain number of symbolic troops under the UN flag. It would seem, what can be more reasonable, if there is a desire to actually reach an agreement and eliminate the hot-beds that from time to time make our relations feverish and sometimes bring them to the red-hot glow.

If there is somebody who is interested in preserving those hot-beds then such interest stems from nothing else but a desire to prevent by all means the normalization of relations between the Soviet Union and the U.S. And I say straightforwardly that it is, of course, Adenauer who is interested in that in the first place. By no means he is motivated by good intentions. The Hitlerite Germany lost the war with all the ensuing consequences. Its plans to expand

"Lebensraum" at the expense of other states ended in failure. This should be recognized once and for all. In fact, that is what the United States, Britain, France, the Soviet Union and other countries fought for against the Hitlerite Germany. Why then should you and we now reckon with the revanchist strivings of the FRG and even encourage them delaying indefinitely the conclusion of a German peace treaty and preserving the present indefinite situation, fraught with danger? After all it is the absence of a peace treaty that feeds the hopes of aggressive revanchist circles in West Germany for a possibility to revise the results of World War II.

Now in all countries there are more and more people who think of and are concerned with the destinies of the world and who seek not to let it escalate to war. They more and more clearly understand that it is impossible to postpone any further the conclusion of a German peace treaty and to preserve the present dangerous situation.

During my conversations on all those questions with your Ambassador Thompson I told him that we are ready to take into consideration the circumstances that you are finding yourself in in connection with preparation for congressional elections. Such, evidently, are "traditions" in the United States that in the course of election struggle they forget, carried away by passions, about common sense and begin playing with fire, competing in saying more and louder absurd things that sow danger of world war. In order not to play in such conditions a role of some third force breaking from outside into this struggle between the competing parties we decided to put the German problem, so to say, on ice until the end of the elections. We had in mind that after elections we would resume the dialogue. We were under the impression that we would meet an understanding on the part of the American side, all the more that on many questions relating to German peace settlement a certain rapprochement of our positions has already been achieved that gives hope for a possibility of an agreement.

The only question on which the difference between us still remains is, as we believe, that of the presence of foreign troops in West Berlin. And even not the question of the presence of troops as such because on that we have already made a step in your direction, but only the question — the troops of what countries will be stationed there. You insist that the occupation troops of the U.S., Britain and France continue to stay in West Berlin. But that would not normalize the situation even after the signing of a peace treaty because the main source of friction between our countries — the use of West Berlin under the cover of occupation regime as a NATO base — would remain unremoved. That is why we considered and continue to consider that the best thing under the circumstances would be to station in West Berlin the UN troops. To stabilize the situation in Europe it would be also reasonable to have both German states — the GDR and the FRG — admitted to the UN, so that they normalize at last relations between each other and with other states — members of the UN.

Such is our position. I stated it in detail to Ambassador Thompson who, evidently, informed you about it.

U.S. Aggression against Cuba

Recently I had a talk with your Secretary of the Interior Mr. S. Udall.[Reported in telegram 616 from Moscow, September 7; for text, see volume V.] He made a good impression on me. Our conversation was friendly. And I never expected that at the time I talked with him you would take a decision to request from the Congress an authority to call up 150.000 reservists. Motivating that step of yours you referred to the red-hot state of international atmosphere and to a necessity for you in that connection to react promptly to the dangers that may arise in any part of "the free world". Everybody understands that when the President of the U.S. demands an increase in armed forces and explains that demand by an aggravation of the situation, it means that he considers that the situation is aggravated by the other side, that is by us, the Soviet Union. But we haven't done anything that could give a pretext for that. We did not carry out any mobilization, and did not make any threats.

I must tell you straightforwardly, Mr. President, that your statement with threats against Cuba is just an inconceivable step. Under present circumstances, when there exist thermonuclear weapons, your request to the Congress for an authority to call up 150.000 reservists is not only a step making the atmosphere red-hot, it is already a dangerous sign that you want to pour oil in the flame, to extinguish that red-hot glow by mobilizing new military contingents. And that, naturally, forces the other side to respond in kind. What could it lead to, all the more that you consider that the U.S. has the right to attack Cuba whenever it wishes? But nowadays is not the Middle Ages, though even at the time it was considered brigandage, and measures were taken against such actions. And in our time such actions are absolutely unthinkable. That is what made us to come out with the TASS statement and later at the session of the UN General Assembly to qualify your act, to remind of the norms of international law and to say about West Berlin.

If there were no statement by you on Cuba, we, naturally, as Ambassador Thompson and Mr. Udall were told, would not say anything on West Berlin. Your statement forced us to do so.

We regret that this dangerous line is being continued in the United States now. What is going on, for example, in the U.S. Congress? How can one, for example, fail to notice the decision of the House of Representatives to stop giving U.S. aid to any country that trades with Cuba or whose ships are used for trading with Cuba. Isn't that an act of an unpermissible arbitrariness against freedom of international trade, an act of crude interference into domestic affairs of other countries?

Very serious consequences may have the resolution adopted by the U.S. Senate on the Cuban question. The contents of that resolution gives ground to draw a conclusion that the U.S. is evidently ready to assume responsibility for unleashing thermonuclear war. We consider that if what is written in that resolution were actually carried out it would mean the beginning of war because no country can agree with such interpretation of rights, with such arbitrariness. Then there would be no U.N., everything would collapse and roll into abyss as it happened once when the League of Nations collapsed. Who wrecked it then? Japan and Hitler, who quit the League of Nations to untie their hands and start war. And they did start it. Could it be that the US wants to embark on such road?

We would greatly regret if it were so. We still do not lose hope that we will be able to normalize our relations. But this can be achieved only when the United States and its allies will strictly adhere to the generally recognized norms of international law and will not interfere into the domestic affairs of other states, will not threaten other countries. This is the main thing. And this is the coexistence of which we spoke more than once. You spoke of it too. But what kind of coexistence is this if the United States would attack countries whose government or socio-political system are not to its liking? In our time the world has split into two camps — capitalist and socialist: you have neighbours whom, as you say, you do not like while we have neighbours whom we do not like, but they are your friends and allies. How can one, especially under these circumstances, consider it to be one's right to attack another country merely because its government and internal order are not to your liking? If we conduct such a policy, where this will lead to — to world war.

The most reasonable and the only right policy in our time if we want to ensure peace and to live in peace is the policy of coexistence. And coexistence is first of all recognizing for every people the right to choose its socio-political system and noninterference by states into internal affairs of others. This also directly follows from the U.N. Charter — the Charter which was adopted by our countries who, moreover, are the founding members of the U.N. To interfere into the internal affairs of other states means to undermine the very foundation on which the whole structure of the U.N. is based. One should not wreck the international building which has been created for the task of ensuring peace and peaceful coexistence.

On the state of Soviet-American relations I would also like to express some other considerations.

I spoke, for instance, to Ambassador Thompson of the buzzing of our ships by American planes. On what grounds this buzzing of the ships sailing in international waters is carried on? Moreover, U.S. Navy ships demand that our ship report to them where they go and what cargo they carry. One U.S. Navy ship even attempted to stop our vessel. I told then Mr. Thompson to convey to you, that we protest against this. Soviet ships which follow on the course given to them by the Government have instructions not to yield to any pirate demands in international waters and to proceed on their course even if they are threatened with opening fire. I said then and I repeat — let them try to stop and sink our ships — this will be the beginning of war because we will answer in kind. We have enough of submarines which can defend the honor of the motherland. Our state possesses other means too. You also have similar means. Why then should such provocations be staged, why should we threaten each other?

I was pleased to receive from you, Mr. President, your assurance that you had given strict instructions not to allow buzzing of our ships. But whether you know it or not the assurance you gave me is not being kept. Your planes even now go on buzzing our ships. I can tell you: in August there were 140 cases of such buzzing.

It has just become known that the Puerto-Rican but actually American authorities detained a British ship and arrested the Soviet cargo aboard that ship — sugar that we have bought in Cuba. If such arbitrariness is not stopped, you yourself realize what it can lead to.

Another unpleasant incident took place in connection with which we had to officially and publicly protest — an intrusion into our air space of a U-2 reconnaissance plane in the area of Sakhalia. You explained that it happened by incident. We took this explanation with understanding. Now it is clear that it did not happen by incident because a U-2 plane also appeared over China. Whom does it belong to? They say — to Chiang Kai-shek. But what is Chiang Kai-shek? Chiang Kai-shek is an affiliate of the U.S. Chiang Kai-shek could not purchase the planes because he himself is on the payroll of the U.S. Therefore those were also the actions of the United States.

Evidently, the same line appears in this case showing that the U.S. has taken a dangerous course. This makes us apprehensive and we are now compelled to take appropriate measures. We did not carry out mobilization and we do not think of one but we have been compelled to order our armed forces to be in peak combat readiness. You forced us to do that by your mobilization and by other measures that you have taken recently.

It may be that all this is being done in connection with pre-election situation in your country. But this is very dangerous. This already goes beyond the limits of the situation within one country because such actions make the international situation red-hot, create a dangerous situation which cannot but cause deep anxiety on the part of the peoples of all countries for the destinies of peace.

It is not pleasant for me, Mr. President, to tell you about it. It would be better, of course, to talk about more pleasant things. But nothing can be done — my position obliges me to give due appraisal of those actions which are now being taken by the United States. We cannot close our eyes and pretend that we do not notice it or do not understand it.

Therefore I would ask you to correctly understand our anxiety and not to do anything that could further aggravate the atmosphere and even expose the world. We on our part again say to you that we will do nothing with regard to West Berlin until the elections in the U.S. After the elections, apparently in the second half of November, it would be necessary in our opinion to continue the dialogue. Of great importance for finding the ways to solve both this problem and other pressing international problems are personal contacts of statesmen on the highest level. I think that if we, persons entrusted with great confidence and bearing enormous responsibility, constantly feel this responsibility, we will have to come to the realization of the necessity of reaching an agreement on West Berlin to eliminate this dangerous hot-bed which spoils our relations all the time.

Moscow, September 28, 1962

In Response to U.S. threats of war over Cuban armaments

The following letter was written to US President John F Kennedy

Mr. President,

I have just received your letter, and have also acquainted myself with text of your speech of October 22 regarding Cuba.

I should say frankly that the measures outlined in your statement represent a serious threat to peace and security of nations. The United States has openly taken a path of gross violations of the Charter of the United Nations, a path violating the international norms of free navigation on the high seas, a path of aggressive actions both against Cuba and against the Soviet Union.

The statement of the United States Government cannot be evaluated in any other way than as naked interference in the domestic affairs of the Cuban Republic, the Soviet Union, and other states. The Charter of United Nations and international norms do not give the right to any state whatsoever to establish, in international waters, control over vessels bound for the shores of the Cuban Republic.

It is self-evident that we also cannot recognize the right of United States to establish control over armaments essential to the Republic of Cuba for the strengthening of its defensive capacity.

We confirm that armaments now en route to Cuba, regardless of the classification to which they belong, are intended exclusively for defensive purposes, in order to secure the Cuban Republic from attack by an aggressor.

I hope that the Government of the United States will show prudence and renounce the actions pursued by you, which could lead to catastrophic consequences for peace throughout world.

The viewpoint of the Soviet Government with regard to your statement of October 22 is set forth in the statement of the Soviet Government, which is being conveyed to you through your Ambassador in Moscow.

Moscow, October 23, 1962.

U.S.: Pushing Mankind Toward the Abyss of a World Nuclear-Missile War

The following letter was written to US President John F Kennedy

Dear Mr President,

I have received your letter of October 23, have studied it, and am answering you.

Just imagine, Mr. President, that we had presented you with the conditions of an ultimatum which you have presented us by your action. How would you have reacted to this? I think that you would have been indignant at such a step on our part. And this would have been understandable to us.

In presenting us with these conditions, you, Mr. President, have flung a challenge at us. Who asked you to do this? By what right did you do this? Our ties with the Republic of Cuba, like our relations with other states, regardless of what kind of states they may be, concern only the two countries between which these relations exist. And if we now speak of the quarantine to which your letter refers, a quarantine may be established, according to accepted international practice, only by agreement of states between themselves, and not by some third party. Quarantines exist, for example, on agricultural goods and products. But in this case the question is in no way one of quarantine, but rather of far more serious things, and you yourself understand this.

You, Mr. President, are not declaring a quarantine, but rather are setting forth an ultimatum and threatening that if we do not give in to your demands you will use force. Consider what you are saying! And you want to persuade me to agree to this! What would it mean to agree to these demands? It would mean guiding oneself in one's relations with other countries not by reason, but by submitting to arbitrariness. You are no longer appealing to reason, but wish to intimidate us.

No, Mr. President, I cannot agree to this, and I think that in your own heart you recognize that I am correct. I am convinced that in my place you would act the same way.

Reference to the decision of the Organization of American States cannot in any way substantiate the demands now advanced by the United States. This Organization has absolutely no authority or basis for adopting decisions such as the one you speak of in your letter. Therefore, we do not recognize these decisions. International law exists and universally recognized norms of conduct exist. We firmly adhere to the principles of international law and observe strictly the norms which regulate navigation on the high seas, in international waters. We observe these norms and enjoy the rights recognized by all states.

You wish to compel us to renounce the rights that every sovereign state enjoys, you are trying to legislate in questions of international law, and you are violating the universally accepted norms of that law. And you are doing all this not only out of hatred for the Cuban people and its government, but also because of considerations of the election campaign in the United States. What morality, what law can justify such an approach by the American Government to international affairs? No such morality or law can be found, because the actions of the United States with regard to Cuba constitute outright banditry or, if you like, the folly of degenerate imperialism. Unfortunately, such folly can bring grave suffering to the peoples of all countries, and to no lesser degree to the American people themselves, since the United States has completely lost its former isolation with the advent of modern types of armament.

Therefore, Mr. President, if you coolly weigh the situation which has developed, not giving way to passions, you will understand that the Soviet Union cannot fail to reject the arbitrary demands of the United States. When you confront us with such conditions, try to put yourself in our place and consider how the United States would react to these conditions. I do not doubt that if someone attempted to dictate similar conditions to you–the United States–you would reject such an attempt. And we also say–no.

The Soviet Government considers that the violation of the freedom to use international waters and international air space is an act of aggression which pushes mankind toward the abyss of a world nuclear-missile war. Therefore, the Soviet Government cannot instruct the captains of Soviet vessels bound for Cuba to observe the orders of American naval forces blockading that Island. Our instructions to Soviet mariners are to observe strictly the universally accepted norms of navigation in international waters and not to retreat one step from them. And if the American side violates these rules, it must realize what responsibility will rest upon it in that case. Naturally we will not simply be bystanders with regard to piratical acts by American ships on the high seas. We will then be forced on our part to take the measures we consider necessary and adequate in order to protect our rights. We have everything necessary to do so.

Moscow, October 24, 1962

Be Sensible — We Want Peace

The following letter was written to US President John F Kennedy

Dear Mr. President:

I have received your letter of October 25. From your letter, I got the feeling that you have some understanding of the situation which has developed and (some) sense of responsibility. I value this.

Now we have already publicly exchanged our evaluations of the events around Cuba and each of us has set forth his explanation and his understanding of these events. Consequently, I would judge that, apparently, a continuation of an exchange of opinions at such a distance, even in the form of secret letters, will hardly add anything to that which one side has already said to the other.

I think you will understand me correctly if you are really concerned about the welfare of the world. Everyone needs peace: both capitalists, if they have not lost their reason, and, still more, Communists, people who know how to value not only their own lives but, more than anything, the lives of the peoples. We,

Communists, are against all wars between states in general and have been defending the cause of peace since we came into the world. We have always regarded war as a calamity, and not as a game nor as a means for the attainment of definite goals, nor, all the more, as a goal in itself. Our goals are clear, and the means to attain them is labor. War is our enemy and a calamity for all the peoples.

It is thus that we, Soviet people, and, together with US, other peoples as well, understand the questions of war and peace. I can, in any case, firmly say this for the peoples of the Socialist countries, as well as for all progressive people who want peace, happiness, and friendship among peoples.

I see, Mr. President, that you too are not devoid of a sense of anxiety for the fate of the world and not without an understanding of what war entails. What would a war give you? You are threatening us with war. But you well know that the very least which you would receive in reply would be that you would experience the same consequences as those which you sent us. And that must be clear to us, people invested with authority, trust, and responsibility. We must not succumb to intoxication and petty passions, regardless of whether elections are impending in this or that country, or not impending. These are all transient things, but if indeed war should break out, then it would not be in our power to stop it, for such is the logic of war. I have participated in two wars and know that war ends when it has rolled through cities and villages, everywhere sowing death and destruction.

In the name of the Soviet Government and the Soviet people, I assure you that your conclusions regarding offensive weapons on Cuba are groundless. It is apparent from what you have written me that our conceptions are different on this score, or rather, we have different estimates of these or those military means. Indeed, in reality, the same forms of weapons can have different interpretations.

You are a military man and, I hope, will understand me. Let us take for example a simple cannon. What sort of means is this: offensive or defensive? A cannon is a defensive means if it is set up to defend boundaries or a fortified area. But if one concentrates artillery, and adds to it the necessary number of troops, then the same cannons do become an offensive means, because they prepare and clear the way for infantry to attack. The same happens with nuclear missile weapons as well, as with any type of this weapon.

You are mistaken if you think that any of our means on Cuba are offensive. However, let us not quarrel now. It is apparent that I will not be able to convince you of this. But I say to you: You, Mr. President, are a military man and should understand: Can one attack, if one has on one's territory even an enormous quantity of missiles of various effective radiuses and various power, but using only these means. These missiles are a means of extermination and destruction. But one cannot attack with these missiles, even nuclear missiles of a power of 100 megatons because only people, troops, can attack. Without people, any means however powerful cannot be offensive.

How can one, consequently, give such a completely incorrect interpretation as you are now giving, to the effect that some sort of means on Cuba are offensive. All the means located there, and I assure you of this, have a defensive character, are on Cuba solely for the purposes of defense, and we have sent them to Cuba at the request of the Cuban Government. You, however, say that these are offensive means.

But, Mr. President, do you really seriously think that Cuba can attack the United States and that even we together with Cuba can attack you from the territory of Cuba? Can you really think that way? How is it possible? We do not understand this. Has something so new appeared in military strategy that one can think that it is possible to attack thus. I say precisely attack, and not destroy, since barbarians, people who have lost their sense, destroy.

I believe that you have no basis to think this way. You can regard us with distrust, but, in any case, you can be calm in this regard, that we are of sound mind and understand perfectly well that if we attack you, you will respond the same way. But you too will receive the same that you hurl against us. And I think that you also understand this. My conversation with you in Vienna gives me the right to talk to you this way.

This indicates that we are normal people, that we correctly understand and correctly evaluate the situation. Consequently, how can we permit the incorrect actions which you ascribe to us? Only lunatics or suicides, who themselves want to perish and to destroy the whole world before they die, could do this. We, however, want to live and do not at all want to destroy your country. We want something quite different: To compete with your country on a peaceful basis. We quarrel with you, we have differences on ideological questions. But our view of the world consists in this, that ideological questions, as well as economic problems, should be solved not by military means, they must be solved on the basis of peaceful competition, i.e., as this is understood in capitalist society, on the basis of competition. We have proceeded and are proceeding from the fact that the peaceful co-existence of the two different social-political systems, now existing in the world, is necessary, that it is necessary to assure a stable peace. That is the sort of principle we hold.

You have now proclaimed piratical measures, which were employed in the Middle Ages, when ships proceeding in international waters were attacked, and you have called this "a quarantine" around Cuba. Our vessels, apparently, will soon enter the zone which your Navy is patrolling. I assure you that these vessels, now bound for Cuba, are carrying the most innocent peaceful cargoes. Do you really think that we only occupy ourselves with the carriage of so-called offensive weapons, atomic and hydrogen bombs? Although perhaps your military people imagine that these (cargoes) are some sort of special type of weapon, I assure you that they are the most ordinary peaceful products.

Consequently, Mr. President, let us show good sense. I

assure you that on those ships, which are bound for Cuba, there are no weapons at all. The weapons which were necessary for the defense of Cuba are already there. I do not want to say that there were not any shipments of weapons at all. No, there were such shipments. But now Cuba has already received the necessary means of defense.

I don't know whether you can understand me and believe me. But I should like to have you believe in yourself and to agree that one cannot give way to passions; it is necessary to control them. And in what direction are events now developing? If you stop the vessels, then, as you yourself know, that would be piracy. If we started to do that with regard to your ships, then you would also be as indignant as we and the whole world now are. One cannot give another interpretation to such actions, because one cannot legalize lawlessness. If this were permitted, then there would be no peace, there would also be no peaceful coexistence. We should then be forced to put into effect the necessary measures of a defensive character to protect our interests in accordance with international law. Why should this be done? To what would all this lead?

Let us normalize relations. We have received an appeal from the Acting Secretary General of the UN, U Thant, with his proposals. I have already answered him. His proposals come to this, that our side should not transport armaments of any kind to Cuba during a certain period of time, while negotiations are being conducted — and we are ready to enter such negotiations — and the other side should not undertake any sort of piratical actions against vessels engaged in navigation on the high seas. I consider these proposals reasonable. This would be a way out of the situation which has been created, which would give the peoples the possibility of breathing calmly. You have asked what happened, what evoked the delivery of weapons to Cuba? You have spoken about this to our Minister of Foreign Affairs. I will tell you frankly, Mr. President, what evoked it.

We were very grieved by the fact — I spoke about it in Vienna — that a landing took place, that an attack on Cuba was committed, as a result of which many Cubans perished. You yourself told me then that this had been a mistake. I respected that explanation. You repeated it to me several times, pointing out that not everybody occupying a high position would acknowledge his mistakes as you had done. I value such frankness. For my part, I told you that we too possess no less courage; we also acknowledged those mistakes which had been committed during the history of our state, and not only acknowledged, but sharply condemned them.

If you are really concerned about the peace and welfare of your people, and this is your responsibility as President, then I, as the Chairman of the Council of Ministers, am concerned for my people. Moreover, the preservation of world peace should be our joint concern, since if, under contemporary conditions, war should break out, it would be a war not only between the reciprocal claims, but a world wide cruel and destructive war.

Why have we proceeded to assist Cuba with military and economic aid? The answer is: We have proceeded to do so only for reasons of humanitarianism. At one time, our people itself had a revolution, when Russia was still a backward country. We were attacked then. We were the target of attack by many countries. The USA participated in that adventure. This has been recorded by participants in the aggression against our country. A whole book has been written about this by General Graves, who, at that time, commanded the US Expeditionary Corps. Graves called it "The American Adventure in Siberia."

We know how difficult it is to accomplish a revolution and how difficult it is to reconstruct a country on new foundations. We sincerely sympathize with Cuba and the Cuban people, but we are not interfering in questions of domestic structure, we are not interfering in their affairs. The Soviet Union desires to help the Cubans build their life as they themselves wish and that others should not hinder them.

You once said that the United States was not preparing an invasion. But you also declared that you sympathized with the Cuban counter-revolutionary emigrants, that you support them and would help them to realize their plans against the present Government of Cuba. It is also not a secret to anyone that the threat of armed attack, aggression, has constantly hung, and continues to hang over Cuba. It was only this which impelled us to respond to the request of the Cuban Government to furnish it aid for the strengthening of the defensive capacity of this country.

If assurances were given by the President and the Government of the United States that the USA itself would not participate in an attack on Cuba and would restrain others from actions of this sort, if you would recall your fleet, this would immediately change everything. I am not speaking for Fidel Castro, but I think that he and the Government of Cuba, evidently, would declare demobilization and would appeal to the people to get down to peaceful labor. Then, too, the question of armaments would disappear, since, if there is no threat, then armaments are a burden for every people. Then too, the question of the destruction, not only of the armaments which you call offensive, but of all other armaments as well, would look different.

I spoke in the name of the Soviet Government in the United Nations and introduced a proposal for the disbandment of all armies and for the destruction of all armaments. How then can I now count on those armaments?

Armaments bring only disasters. When one accumulates them, this damages the economy, and if one puts them to use, then they destroy people on both sides. Consequently, only a madman can believe that armaments are the principal means in the life of society. No, they are an enforced loss of human energy, and what is more are for the destruction of man himself. If people do not show wisdom, then in the final analysis they will come to a clash, like blind moles, and then reciprocal extermination will begin.

Let us therefore show statesmanlike wisdom. I propose: We, for our part, will declare that our ships, bound for Cuba, will not carry any kind of armaments. You would declare that the United States will not invade Cuba with its forces and will not support any sort of forces which might intend to carry out an invasion of Cuba. Then the necessity for the presence of our military specialists in Cuba would disappear.

Mr. President, I appeal to you to weigh well what the aggressive, piratical actions, which you have declared the USA intends to carry out in international waters, would lead to. You yourself know that any sensible man simply cannot agree with this, cannot recognize your right to such actions.

If you did this as the first step towards the unleashing of war, well then, it is evident that nothing else is left to us but to accept this challenge of yours. If, however, you have not lost your self-control and sensibly conceive what this might lead to, then, Mr. President, we and you ought not now to pull on the ends of the rope in which you have tied the knot of war, because the more the two of us pull, the tighter that knot will be tied. And a moment may come when that knot will be tied so tight that even he who tied it will not have the strength to untie it, and then it will be necessary to cut that knot, and what that would mean is not for me to explain to you, because you yourself understand perfectly of what terrible forces our countries dispose.

Consequently, if there is no intention to tighten that knot

and thereby to doom the world to the catastrophe of thermonuclear war, then let us not only relax the forces pulling on the ends of the rope, let us take measures to untie that knot. We are ready for this.

We welcome all forces which stand on positions of peace. Consequently, I expressed gratitude to Mr. Bertrand Russell, too, who manifests alarm and concern for the fate of the world, and I readily responded to the appeal of the Acting Secretary General of the UN, U Thant.

There, Mr. President, are my thoughts, which, if you agreed with them, could put an end to that tense situation which is disturbing all peoples.

These thoughts are dictated by a sincere desire to relieve the situation, to remove the threat of war.

Moscow, October 26, 1962

We Will Remove Our Missiles From Cuba

The following letter was written to US President John F Kennedy

Dear Mr President,

I have studied with great satisfaction your reply to Mr. Thant concerning measures that should be taken to avoid contact between our vessels and thereby avoid irreparable and fatal consequences. This reasonable step on your part strengthens my belief that you are showing concern for the preservation of peace, which I note with satisfaction.

I have already said that our people, our Government, and I personally, as Chairman of the Council of Ministers, are concerned solely with having our country develop and occupy a worthy place among all peoples of the world in economic competition, in the development of culture and the arts, and in raising the living standard of the people. This is the most noble and necessary field for competition, and both the victor and the vanquished will derive only benefit from it, because it means peace and an increase in the means by which man lives and finds enjoyment.

In your statement you expressed the opinion that the main aim was not simply to come to an agreement and take measures to prevent contact between our vessels and consequently a deepening of the crisis which could, as a result of such contacts spark a military conflict, after which all negotiations would be superfluous because other forces and other laws would then come into play–the laws of war. I agree with you that this is only the first step. The main thing that must be done is to normalize and stabilize the state of peace among states and among peoples.

I understand your concern for the security of the United States, Mr. President, because this is the primary duty of a President. But we too are disturbed about these same questions; I bear these same obligations as Chairman of the Council of Ministers of the U.S.S.R. You have been alarmed by the fact that we have aided Cuba with weapons, in order to strengthen its defense capability–precisely defense capability–because whatever weapons it may possess, Cuba cannot be equated with you since the difference in magnitude is so great, particularly in view of modern means of destruction. Our aim has been and is to help Cuba, and no one can dispute the humanity of our motives, which are oriented toward enabling Cuba to live peacefully and develop in the way its people desire.

You wish to ensure the security of your country, and this is understandable. But Cuba, too, wants the same thing; all countries want to maintain their security. But how are we, the Soviet Union, our Government, to assess your actions which are expressed in the fact that you have surrounded the Soviet Union with military bases; surrounded our allies with military bases; placed military bases literally around our country; and stationed your missile armaments there? This is no secret. Responsible American personages openly declare that it is so. Your missiles are located in Britain, are located in Italy, and are aimed against us. Your missiles are located in Turkey.

You are disturbed over Cuba. You say that this disturbs you because it is 90 miles by sea from the coast of the United States of America. But Turkey adjoins us; our sentries patrol back and forth and see each other. Do you consider, then, that you have the right to demand security for your own country and the removal of the weapons you call offensive, but do not accord the same right to us? You have placed destructive missile weapons, which you call offensive, in Turkey, literally next to us. How then can recognition of our equal military capacities be reconciled with such unequal relations between our great states? This is irreconcilable.

It is good, Mr. President, that you have agreed to have our representatives meet and begin talks, apparently through the mediation of U Thant, Acting Secretary General of the United Nations. Consequently, to some degree he has assumed the role of a mediator and we consider that he will be able to cope with this responsible mission, provided, of course, that each party drawn into this controversy displays good will.

I think it would be possible to end the controversy quickly

and normalize the situation, and then the people could breathe more easily, considering that statesmen charged with responsibility are of sober mind and have an awareness of their responsibility combined with the ability to solve complex questions and not bring things to a military catastrophe.

I therefore make this proposal: We are willing to remove from Cuba the means which you regard as offensive. We are willing to carry this out and to make this pledge in the United Nations. Your representatives will make a declaration to the effect that the United States, for its part, considering the uneasiness and anxiety of the Soviet State, will remove its analogous means from Turkey. Let us reach agreement as to the period of time needed by you and by us to bring this about. And, after that, persons entrusted by the United Nations Security Council could inspect on the spot the fulfillment of the pledges made. Of course, the permission of the Governments of Cuba and Turkey is necessary for the entry into those countries of these representatives and for the inspection of the fulfillment of the pledge made by each side. Of course it would be best if these representatives enjoyed the confidence of the Security Council as well as yours and mine—both the United States and the Soviet Union—and also that of Turkey and Cuba. I do not think it would be difficult to select people who would enjoy the trust and respect of all parties concerned.

We, in making this pledge, in order to give satisfaction and hope of the peoples of Cuba and Turkey and to strengthen their confidences in their security, will make a statement within the framework of the Security Council to the effect that the Soviet Government gives a solemn promise to respect the inviolability of the borders and sovereignty of Turkey, not to interfere in its internal affairs, not to invade Turkey, not to make available our territory as a bridgehead for such an invasion, and that it would also restrain those who contemplate committing aggression against Turkey, either from the territory of the Soviet Union or from the territory of Turkey's other neighboring states.

The United States Government will make a similar statement within the framework of the Security Council regarding Cuba. It will declare that the United States will respect the inviolability of Cuba's borders and its sovereignty, will pledge not to interfere in its internal affairs, not to invade Cuba itself or make its territory available as a bridgehead for such an invasion, and will also restrain those who might contemplate committing aggression against Cuba, either from the territory of the United States or from the territory of Cuba's other neighboring states.

Of course, for this we would have to come to an agreement with you and specify a certain time limit. Let us agree to some period of time, but without unnecessary delay–say within two or three weeks, not longer than a month.

The means situated in Cuba, of which you speak and which disturb you, as you have stated, are in the hands of Soviet officers. Therefore, any accidental use of them to the detriment of the United States is excluded. These means are situated in Cuba at the request of the Cuban Government and are only for defense purposes. Therefore, if there is no invasion of Cuba, or attack on the Soviet Union or any of our other allies, then of course these means are not and will not be a threat to anyone. For they are not for purposes of attack.

If you are agreeable to my proposal, Mr. President, then we would send our representatives to New York, to the United Nations, and would give them comprehensive instructions in order that an agreement may be reached more quickly. If you also select your people and give them the corresponding instructions, then this question can be quickly resolved.

Why would I like to do this? Because the whole world is now apprehensive and expects sensible actions of us. The greatest joy for all peoples would be the announcement of our agreement and of the eradication of the controversy that has arisen. I attach great importance to this agreement in so far as it could serve as a good beginning and could in particular make it easier to reach agreement on banning nuclear weapons tests. The question of the tests could be solved in parallel fashion, without connecting one with the other, because these are different issues. However, it is important that agreement be reached on both these issues so as to present humanity with a fine gift, and also to gladden it with the news that agreement has been reached on the cessation of nuclear tests and that consequently the atmosphere will no longer be poisoned. Our position and yours on this issue are very close together.

All of this could possibly serve as a good impetus toward the finding of mutually acceptable agreements on other controversial issues on which you and I have been exchanging views. These issues have so far not been resolved, but they are awaiting urgent solution, which would clear up the international atmosphere. We are prepared for this.

These are my proposals, Mr. President.

Moscow, October 27, 1962